W9-BMG-704

DREYER'S ENGLISH

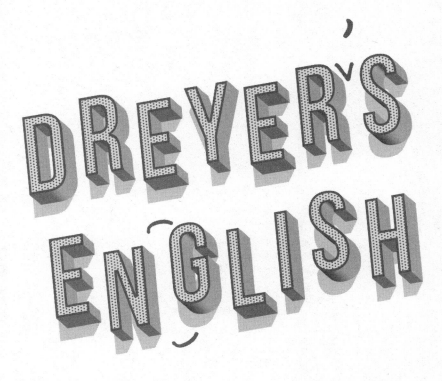

DREYER'S ENGLISH

Good Advice for Good Writing

(Adapted for Young Readers)

BENJAMIN DREYER

Delacorte Press

Text copyright © 2021 by Benjamin Dreyer

All rights reserved. Published in the United States by Delacorte Press, an imprint of
Random House Children's Books, a division of Penguin Random House LLC, New York.

This work is based on *Dreyer's English: An Utterly Correct Guide to Clarity and Style,*
copyright © 2019 by Benjamin Dreyer. Published in the United States in hardcover by
Random House, an imprint and division of Penguin Random House LLC, New York,
in 2019.

Delacorte Press is a registered trademark and the colophon is a trademark
of Penguin Random House LLC.

Visit us on the Web! rhcbooks.com

Educators and librarians, for a variety of teaching tools, visit us at
RHTeachersLibrarians.com

Library of Congress Cataloging-in-Publication Data is available upon request.
ISBN 978-0-593-17680-1 (trade) — ISBN 978-0-593-17681-8 (lib. bdg.) —
ISBN 978-0-593-17682-5 (ebook) — ISBN 978-0-593-37712-3 (international edition)

The text of this book is set in 12-point Sabon LT.
Interior design by Ken Crossland

Jacket lettering used under license from Shutterstock.com

Printed in Canada
10 9 8 7 6 5 4 3 2 1
First Edition

For my family: Diana, Nancy,
Gabe, Robert, and Sallie

And in memory of my father,
Stanley B. Dreyer (1925–2020)

"You should say what you mean," the March Hare went on.

"I do," Alice hastily replied; "at least—at least I mean what I say—that's the same thing, you know."

"Not the same thing a bit!" said the Hatter. "Why, you might just as well say that 'I see what I eat' is the same thing as 'I eat what I see'!"

"You might just as well say," added the March Hare, "that 'I like what I get' is the same thing as 'I get what I like'!"

—LEWIS CARROLL,
Alice's Adventures in Wonderland

CONTENTS

INTRODUCTION

BY WAY OF INTRODUCTION

I am a copy editor. After a piece of writing has been, likely through numerous drafts, developed and revised by the writer and by the person I tend to call the *editor* editor and deemed essentially finished and complete, my job is to lay my hands on that piece of writing and make it . . . better. Cleaner. Clearer. More efficient. Not to rewrite it, not to bully and flatten it into some notion of Correct Prose, whatever that might be, but to burnish and polish it and make it the best possible version of itself that it can be—to make it read even more like itself than it did when I got to work on it.

Fascinating, you say, but I'm not a copy editor. I'm a student. I write essays and reports and blog posts and maybe the occasional short story. No one cares if my emails have been polished. My friends know what I mean.

And that's probably true. Your friends don't think

twice when you text them using mostly emojis and capital letters with no vowels. But what if—stay with me—what if you don't communicate with *just these people* for the rest of your life? What if you need to make yourself understood, clearly, by a professor or a boss or a customer or a lawyer? What if you want to impress a potential employer or publisher? Yes, there's spellcheck, and those squiggly lines you mostly ignore that mean something isn't perfect with your grammar. If you're lucky, you can figure out what they mean and make adjustments. But those tools can't fix everything. Spellcheck and autocorrect are marvelous helps—I never type without one or the other turned on—but they won't always get you to the word you meant to use.

What you write and how you write it tells readers as much about you as a selfie. You don't post every selfie you take, do you? You pick the ones that present to the world the person you want to be. Your writing does the same thing; why not show your best self? Just as there are unwritten dress codes for various life events—what you wear to a basketball game or a movie versus what you wear to a fancy restaurant or a funeral—there are times when it's perfectly acceptable to write in casual shorthand, and there are times when it's not.

Don't let the word "copyediting" make you nervous. Think of it as revising or refining. Whatever you call it, the process involves shaking loose and rearranging punctuation—I sometimes feel as if I spend half my life prying up commas and the other half tacking them down someplace else—and keeping an eye open for dropped words ("He went to store") and repeated words ("He went to the the store") and other glitches. In most cases, you want to obey the basic rules of grammar—applied more formally for some writing, like schoolwork; less formally for other writing, like fiction.

Beyond this is where copyediting can elevate itself from what sounds like something a passably sophisticated piece of software should be able to accomplish—it can't, not for style, not for grammar (even if it thinks it can), and not for spelling (more on spelling, much more on spelling, later)—to a true craft. On a good day, it achieves something between a really thorough teeth cleaning—as a writer once described it to me—and a whiz-bang magic act.

• • •

Which brings me to you, dear reader—I've always wanted to say that, "dear reader," and now, having said it, I promise never to say it again—and why we're here.

We're all of us writers: We write term papers and letters to teachers and product reviews, journals and blog entries, appeals to politicians. Some of us write books. All of us write emails.* And, at least as I've observed it, we all want to do it better: We want to make our points more clearly, more elegantly; we want our writing to be appreciated, to be more effective; we want—to be quite honest—to make fewer mistakes.

This book, then, is my chance to share with you, for your own use, some of what I do, from the nuts-and-bolts stuff that even skilled writers stumble over to some of the fancy little tricks I've come across or devised that can make even skilled writing better.

Let's get started.

No. Wait. Before we get started:

The reason this book is not called *The Last Style Manual You'll Ever Need,* or something equally ghastly, is because it's not. Style manuals, also called stylebooks, are

---

* We also text and tweet, and these activities have spawned their own rules, which is that there are very few rules. Don't be fooled: Texting and tweeting are not reliable ways of making yourself universally understood. Anyone not familiar with the social media world will have no idea what you mean if you write IDK TTYL when you email them. And if you don't care because who's not familiar with the social media world?, then consider the following, from *I Am Not Your Perfect Mexican Daughter,* by Erika L. Sánchez: "Standard English . . . is the language of power. . . . It means that you . . . speak and write in a way that will give you authority. Does that mean that the way you speak in your neighborhood is wrong? That slang is bad? . . . Absolutely not. That form of speaking is often fun, inventive, and creative, but would it be helpful to speak that way in a job interview? Unfortunately not."

guides that offer best practices on questions of grammar and language. Two common stylebooks you'll encounter in the publishing industry are *The Chicago Manual of Style* and *Words into Type*. They're both comprehensive enough to cover just about everything you'll need at this point in your writing life, and you'll find more of my picks in Things I Like on page 267. But here's the rub: No single stylebook can ever tell you everything you want to know about writing—no two stylebooks, I might add, can ever agree on everything you want to know about writing—and in setting out to write this book, I settled on my own ground rules: (1) that I would write about the issues I most often run across while copyediting and how I attempt to address them, about topics where I think I truly have something to add to the conversation, and about curiosities that interest or simply amuse me, and (2) that I would not attempt to replicate the guidance of the exhaustive books that still and always will sit, and be constantly referred to, on my own desk.*

---

* For the record: *Of course* you need to own a dictionary. Get yourself a copy of *Merriam-Webster's Collegiate Dictionary*—in its eleventh edition, as of this writing. Professional copy editors will also never be without *Words into Type,* a splendid volume that long ago went out of print but copies of which are relatively easily found online, and *The Chicago Manual of Style,* whose edicts I don't always agree with but whose definitive bossiness is, in its way, comforting.

And, I should add, that I would remember, at least every now and then, to own up to my own specific tastes and noteworthy eccentricities and allow that just because I think something is good and proper you don't necessarily have to.

Though you should.

PART 1

THE STUFF
IN THE FRONT

CHAPTER 1

THE LIFE-CHANGING MAGIC
OF TIDYING UP (YOUR PROSE)

Here's your first challenge:
Go a week without writing the words

- very
- kind of/sort of
- really
- totally

And you can toss in—or, that is, toss out—"just" (not in the sense of "righteous" but in the sense of "merely") and "so" (in the "extremely" sense, though as conjunctions go it's pretty disposable too).

Oh yes: "pretty." As in "pretty tedious." Go ahead and kill that particular darling.

And "of course." That's right out. And "surely." And "that said."

And "actually"? Feel free to go the rest of your life without another "actually."*

If you can go a week without writing any of what I've come to think of as the Wan Intensifiers and Throat Clearers—I wouldn't ask you to go a week without *saying* them; that would render most people silent—you will at the end of that week be a considerably better writer than you were at the beginning. The Wan Intensifiers add nothing. Avoid them.

I wouldn't necessarily call that a rule of good writing; writing isn't always about rules. That said, I have nothing against rules. They're indispensable when playing Monopoly or chess, and their observance can go a long way toward improving a ride on the subway. The rule of law? Big fan.

The English language, though, is not so easily ruled and regulated. It developed without codification, sucking up new constructions and vocabulary every time some foreigner set foot on the British Isles—to say nothing of the mischief we Americans have wreaked on it these last few centuries—and continues to evolve anarchically. It has, to my great dismay, no enforceable laws, much less someone to enforce the laws it doesn't have.

---

* "Actually" has been a weakness of mine my entire life, speaking and writing, and I realized that it was contagious the first time I heard my two-year-old nephew declare, "Actually, I like peas."

Certain prose rules are essentially inarguable—that a sentence's subject and its verb should agree in number, for instance. Or that in a "not only x but y" construction, the x and the y must be parallel elements. (More on this in Chapter 4: A Little Grammar Is a Dangerous Thing.) Why? I suppose because these prose rules are firmly entrenched, because no one cares to argue with them, and because they help us use our words to their best purpose: to communicate clearly with our readers. Let's call these reasons the Four C's: Convention. Consensus. Clarity. Comprehension.

Also simply because a well-constructed sentence sounds better. Literally sounds better. One of the best ways to determine whether your writing is well constructed is to read it aloud. A sentence that can't readily be spoken is a sentence that likely needs to be rewritten.

A good sentence, I find myself saying frequently, is one that the reader can follow from beginning to end, no matter how long it is, without having to double back in confusion because the writer misused or omitted a key piece of punctuation, chose a vague or misleading pronoun, or in some other way engaged in inadvertent misdirection.

As much as I like a good rule, I'm an enthusiastic subscriber to the notion of "rules are meant to be broken"—once you've learned them, I hasten to add.

Right now, let's attend to a few of what I think of as the Great Nonrules of the English Language. You've encountered all of these; you've probably been taught them in school. I'd like you to free yourself of them. They're not helping you; all they're doing is clogging your brain, making you look self-consciously over your own shoulder as you write. And once you've done that, once you've gotten rid of these nonrules, hopefully* you can pay attention to more important things.

Why are they nonrules? So far as I'm concerned, because they're largely unhelpful, pointlessly constricting, ill-considered, and useless. Also because they're generally of questionable origin: devised out of thin air, then passed on till they've gained respectable solidity and the ring of authority. Language experts have done their best to get rid of them, but these made-up strictures refuse to go away and have proven more durable than cat videos. Part of the problem, I must add, is that some of them were made up by self-proclaimed but presumably well-meaning language experts in the first place, so getting rid of them can be a bit like trying to get a dog to stop chasing its own tail.

---

* Oh, yes indeed. I'll meet you in Chapter 7: Pet Peeves.

The Big Three

1. Never Begin a Sentence with "And" or "But."

No, *do* begin a sentence with "And" or "But," if it strikes your fancy to do so. Great writers do it all the time. So do even not-necessarily-great writers, like the person who has, so far in this book, done it a few times and intends to do it a lot more.

But first a warning:

An "And" or a "But" (or a "For" or an "Or" or a "However" or a "Because," to cite four other sentence starters you might often be warned against) is not always the strongest beginning for a sentence, and making a habit of using any of them can make your writing boring and lazy. You may find that you don't need that "And" at all. You may find that your "And" or "But" sentence will easily attach to the sentence before it with a comma or even, if you're brave, a semicolon. Take a good look, and give it a good think.[*]

Let's test an example or two.

> Francie, of course, became an outsider shunned by all because of her stench. But she had become accustomed to being lonely.

---

[*] I'm always on my guard for monotonous repetition, whether it's of a pet word—all writers have pet words—or a pet sentence construction. Two sentences in a single paragraph beginning with the same introductory term, especially "But," are usually one sentence too many.

> Francie, of course, became an outsider shunned
> by all because of her stench, but she had
> become accustomed to being lonely.

Which do you think Betty Smith, the author of *A Tree Grows in Brooklyn,* chose? The former, as it happens. Had I been Smith's copy editor, I might well have suggested the second, to make one coherent, connected thought out of two unnecessarily separated ones. Perhaps she'd have agreed, or perhaps she'd have preferred the text as she'd written it, hearing it in her head as a solemn knell, a heavy note of sadness. That period does give the second sentence some extra weight, doesn't it. And authors do often prefer their text the way they've written it.[*]

See what I mean about how these nonrules unnecessarily complicate and restrict your writing? You can choose to ignore them—writing is about making conscious, careful choices, and choosing is how you build a book—or a story or a book report.

One thing to add: Writers who are not so adept at

---

[*] I admit that it's not entirely fair of me to present two isolated sentences and make a ruling about them. When you read, you're listening to the text not only sentence by sentence but also paragraph by paragraph and page by page, for a larger sense of sweep and rhythm, a lot like the way you listen to a song for its beat and how it makes you feel, not just for those two lines in the refrain that don't mean anything.

linking their sentences habitually toss in a "But" or a "However" to create the illusion that a second thought contradicts a first thought when it doesn't do any such thing. It doesn't work, and I'm on to you.

2. Never Split an Infinitive.

To cite a famous split infinitive—and everyone cites this bit from the original *Star Trek* TV series, so zero points to me for originality—"To boldly go where no man has gone before."*

There's much more—*much more*—I could say on the subject, but I don't want to write about the nineteenth-century textual critic Henry Alford any more than you want to read about the nineteenth-century textual critic Henry Alford, so let's leave it at this: A split infinitive, as we generally understand the term, is a "to [verb]" construction with an adverb stuck in the middle of it. In the *Star Trek* example, then, an unsplit infinitive version would be "Boldly to go where no man has gone before" or "To go boldly where no man has gone before." If either of those sounds better to you, be my guest. To me they sound as if they were translated from the Vulcan.

---

* Later and wisely rewritten to "To boldly go where no one has gone before."

3. Never End a Sentence with a Preposition.

This is the rule that invariably (and wearily) leads to a rehash of the celebrated remark by British prime minister Winston Churchill that British prime minister Winston Churchill, in reality, neither said nor wrote:

"This is the kind of arrant pedantry up with which I will not put." Meaning, basically, this rule is bogus and I'm not going to follow it, because that's how you end up with monstrous sentences.

Let me say this about this: Ending a sentence with a preposition ("as," "at," "by," "for," "from," "of," etc.) isn't always such a hot idea, mostly because a sentence should aim for a powerful finale and not simply dribble off like a rusty old playground water fountain. A sentence that meanders its way to a prepositional finish is often weaker than it ought to or could be.

What did you do that for?

is passable, but

Why did you do that?

has some snap to it.

Still, to tie a sentence into a strangling knot to avoid a prepositional conclusion is unhelpful and unnatural, and it's something no good writer should attempt and no eager reader should have to contend with.

See what I just did?

The Lesser Seven

I'm sure there are many more secondary nonrules than these seven, but these are the ones I'm most often asked about (or challenged on), so:

1. Contractions Aren't Allowed in Formal Writing.

This may be a fine rule to observe if you want to sound as if you learned English on your native Mars, but there's not a goshdarn thing wrong with "don't," "can't," "wouldn't," and all the rest of them that people naturally use, and without them many a piece of writing would turn out stilted and wooden. The likes of "I'd've" and "should've" may be too loosey-goosey outside casual prose, but generally speaking: Contractions are why we invented the apostrophe, so make good use of both.

Speaking of "should've":

If you want to convey the particular sound of a particular character's speech—and I warn you, I will have more to say later about the dangers of phonetic dialogue—please use "should've," "could've," "would've," and so forth. Don't try to get creative with "shoulduv," "coulduv," "woulduv," or some other made-up spelling. They sound precisely the same as the regular spelling, so use the regular spelling and no one will yell at you and we'll all be a lot happier.

2. The Passive Voice Is to Be Avoided.

A sentence written in the passive voice is one whose subject would, in a sentence constructed in the active voice, be its object. That is:

Active Voice: The clown terrified us.
Passive Voice: We were terrified by the clown.

In a sentence written in the passive voice, the thing that is acted upon is frontloaded, and the thing doing the acting comes at the end. In either case, we can easily agree that clowns are terrifying.

Often, in a sentence constructed in the passive voice, the actor is omitted entirely. Sometimes this is done in an attempt to call attention to a problem without laying blame ("The refrigerator door was left open") and sometimes, in weasel-like fashion, to avoid taking responsibility: "Mistakes were made," for instance.

Here's a nifty trick that comes in handy when you're assessing your own writing:

If you can add "by zombies" to the end of a sentence

(or, yes, "by the clown"), you've written a sentence in the passive voice.

All this said, there's nothing wrong with sentences constructed in the passive voice—you're simply choosing where you want to put the sentence's emphasis—and I see nothing objectionable in, say,

> The floors were swept, the beds made, the rooms aired out.

since the point of interest is the cleanness of the house and not the identity of the cleaner.

But many a sentence can be improved by putting its true protagonist at the beginning, so that's something to be considered.[*]

3. Sentence Fragments. They're Bad.

I give you one of my favorite novel openers of all time, that of Charles Dickens's *Bleak House:*

> London. Michaelmas Term lately over, and the Lord Chancellor sitting in Lincoln's Inn Hall. Implacable November weather. As much mud in the streets as if the waters had but

---

[*] By zombies.

newly retired from the face of the earth, and
it would not be wonderful to meet a Megalo-
saurus, forty feet long or so, waddling like an
elephantine lizard up Holborn Hill. Smoke
lowering down from chimney-pots, making a soft black drizzle, with flakes of soot
in it as big as full-grown snow-flakes—gone
into mourning, one might imagine, for the
death of the sun. Dogs, undistinguishable
in mire. Horses, scarcely better; splashed to
their very blinkers. Foot passengers, jostling
one another's umbrellas in a general infection of ill-temper, and losing their foot-hold
at street-corners, where tens of thousands
of other foot passengers have been slipping
and sliding since the day broke (if this day
ever broke), adding new deposits to the crust
upon crust of mud, sticking at those points
tenaciously to the pavement, and accumulat-
ing at compound interest.

Fog everywhere. Fog up the river, where
it flows among green aits and meadows; fog
down the river, where it rolls defiled among
the tiers of shipping, and the waterside pol-
lutions of a great (and dirty) city. Fog on the
Essex marshes, fog on the Kentish heights.

Fog creeping into the cabooses of collier-brigs; fog lying out on the yards, and hovering in the rigging of great ships; fog drooping on the gunwales of barges and small boats. Fog in the eyes and throats of ancient Greenwich pensioners, wheezing by the firesides of their wards; fog in the stem and bowl of the afternoon pipe of the wrathful skipper, down in his close cabin; fog cruelly pinching the toes and fingers of his shivering little 'prentice boy on deck. Chance people on the bridges peeping over the parapets into a nether sky of fog, with fog all round them, as if they were up in a balloon, and hanging in the misty clouds.

A, Isn't that great? Don't you want to run off and read the whole novel now? Do it! I'll wait here for three months. B, Please count that excerpt's complete sentences, and let me know when you get beyond zero.*

You may not be Charles Dickens, but a well-wielded sentence fragment (or, as here, a whole bunch of them) can be a delightful thing. It's another example of the conscious choices you make in writing—it's one thing to artfully

---

* You could argue that the second half of the bit beginning "As much mud" constitutes a complete and freestanding sentence. I'm not in the mood to make that argument, but you feel free.

create a scene and an atmosphere with your fragments; it's another entirely to lazily punctuate unrelated thoughts. Wield your fragments with a purpose, and mindfully. Otherwise they can end up sounding like asthma.

4. A Person Must Be a "Who."

I don't know why violation of this nonrule flips some people out, but it does, and they can get loudly cranky about it.

So just as loudly: A person can be a "that."

The guy who wrote "You're the One That I Want" from *Grease* knew precisely what he was doing. The one that I want, the teachers that attended the conference, the whoevers that whatevered.

A thing, by the way, can also be a "who," as in "an idea whose time has come," because you certainly don't want to be writing "an idea the time of which has come," or worse. (Though worse might not exist.)

5. "None" Is Singular.

If you can find fault with the sentence "None of us are going to the party," you have an ear better attuned to the English language than mine.

"None" can certainly be used singularly, if that which is to be emphasized is a collection of discrete individuals: "None of the suspects, it seems, is guilty of the crime." But if you mean to emphasize the feelings, or actions, or inactions, of a group *as a group*, go ahead and use the plural: "None of them are guilty."

6. "Whether" Must Never Be Accompanied by "Or Not."

In many sentences, particularly those in which the word "whether" is being used as a straight-up "if," no "or not" is called for.

> Not only do I not care *what* you think, I don't care *whether* you think.

But see as well:

> Whether or not you like movie musicals, I'm sure you'll love *Pitch Perfect*.

Try deleting the "or not" from that sentence and see what happens.

That's the whole thing: If you can delete the "or not" from a "whether or not" and your sentence continues to make sense, then go ahead and delete it. If not, don't.

7. Never Introduce a List with "Like."

"Great writers of the twenty-first century like Louis Sachar, Rebecca Stead, and Lois Lowry . . ."

Screech of brakes as a squad car of grammar police pulls that burgeoning sentence to the side of the road and demands that "like" be replaced with "such as."

I confess to some guilt here, as I had it drummed into my head that inclusive lists should be introduced exclusively with "such as," and that to start such a list with "like" suggests comparison. By that logic, in the example above, Sachar, Stead, and Lowry may be *like* great twenty-first-century writers but are not *themselves* great twenty-first-century writers.

But who could possibly read such a sentence and think such a thing?

And that's often the problem, isn't it? In writing and in so many things: that we accept things we're taught without thinking about them at all.

This particular nonrule, I eventually learned and you may be pleased to note, sprung up[*] only as recently as the mid-twentieth century, and it has little foundation in anything other than personal preference.

That said, there's nothing wrong with the slightly more grand-sounding "such as." But feel free to like "like."

---

[*] Hold on there, People Who Think They Know Better and Write Aggrieved Emails to Publishing Houses. "Sprung" rather than "sprang" is perfectly correct. Look it up.

CHAPTER 2

56 ASSORTED THINGS TO DO (AND NOT TO DO) WITH PUNCTUATION

If words are the flesh, muscle, and bone of prose, punctuation is the breath. In support of the words you've carefully selected, punctuation is your best means of conveying to the reader how you want your writing to be read, how you want it to sound. A comma sounds different than a semicolon; parentheses make a different noise than dashes.

Some writers use punctuation with impressionistic flair, and as a copy editor I do my best to support that, so long as the result is comprehensible and consistent. Not all punctuation is a choice, though. Typing or not typing even so much as a comma—in fact, especially a comma—can convey key information. Make sure you use punctuation wisely.

Periods

1.

Those two-letter state abbreviations that the USPS—which I'm still tempted to style U.S.P.S. but won't—likes to see on envelopes (MA, NY, CA, and the like) do not take periods. They also shouldn't appear anywhere else but on envelopes and packages. In bibliographies and notes sections, and anywhere else you may need to abbreviate a state's name, please stick to the old-fashioned and more attractive Mass., N.Y., Calif., and so on. Or just write the whole thing out.

2.

Some of us have a hard time dropping the periods from the abbreviation U.S., perhaps simply out of habit, perhaps because US looks to us like the (shouted) objective case of "we." Some of us were also taught to use U.S. (or that other thing) only as an adjective, as in "U.S. foreign policy," and to refer to the country nounwise only full-out as the United States. I persist in that distinction, because . . . because I do.

3.

Feel free to end a sentence shaped like a question that isn't really a question with a period rather than a question mark. It makes a statement, doesn't it.

Commas

4.

The series comma is the comma that separates the last two bits in a list of words or phrases before the concluding conjunction "and" or "or" or sometimes even "but," as in:

> apples, pears, oranges, tangerines, tangelos,
> bananas, and cherries

The "bananas, and" comma. That's the series comma.

You may know this comma as the Oxford comma—because, we're told, it's traditionally favored by the editors at Oxford University Press, a well-respected and well-established publisher of Very Smart People. But as a patriotic American, I'm loath to perpetuate that policy. Or you may be familiar with the term "serial comma," though for me "serial" evokes "killer," so no again.

Whatever you want to call it: Use it. I don't want to belabor the point; neither am I willing to negotiate it.

No sentence has ever been harmed by a series comma, and many a sentence has been improved by one.

5.

Exception to the rule: An ampersand (&) in a series rather than an "and"—this sort of thing tends to turn up in book or film titles, the names of law firms (and other companies that want to invest themselves with the cachet of law firms), and nowhere else, but it's a thing to know—negates the necessity of a series comma, mostly because the result would be unsightly. Thus, oh, say:

> *Eats, Shoots & Leaves* [a popular book on
> punctuation by Lynne Truss]

and certainly not

> *Eats, Shoots, & Leaves*

6.

You might well, if you're relatively sparing with your commas, write

> On Friday she went to school.

or

> Last week Laurence visited his grandmother.

So long as the commaless rendition is clear and understandable, you're on safe ground.

The longer the introductory bit, the more likely you are to want/need a comma:

> After three days home sick with a stomachache,
>   she returned to school.
> On his way back from basketball practice,
>   Laurence visited his grandmother.

7.

But do avoid crashing proper nouns, as in

> In June Trump's personal lawyer spoke to
>   representatives in Moscow.

Lest you want your reader wondering who June Trump is and what precisely got into her attorney.

Or consider a sentence that begins, say, "On arrival at Random House I was informed," which might set you, if only for a millisecond, to speculating about Random House II and Random House III.

8.

Sometimes a comma makes no sense at all.

> Suddenly, he ran from the room.

Makes it all rather less sudden, doesn't it.

9.

A comma splice is the use of a comma to join two sentences when each can stand on its own—as in:

> I don't know why it's a problem for you, I just
> like unicorns.

As a rule you should avoid comma splicing, though exceptions can be and frequently are made when the individual sentences are reasonably short and intimately connected: "I came, I saw, I conquered" or "Your strengths are your weaknesses, your weaknesses are your strengths." Another exception arises in fiction or fictionlike writing in which such a splice may be effective in linking closely related thoughts or expressing hurried action and even a semicolon—more on the glorious semicolon below—is more pause than is desired.

An example, from Walter Baxter's undeservedly obscure 1951 novel *Look Down in Mercy:*

> He had never noticed [the sunset] before, it
> seemed fantastically beautiful.

As comma splices go, this one's not doing anyone any harm, and there's no issue here with comprehension, so let's let it go.

The result of a comma splice is known as a run-on sentence. You may meet a fair number of people who like to aim that term at any old sentence that happens to be long and twisty and made up of a bunch of bits divided by semicolons, dashes, parentheses, and whatever else the writer may have had on hand. Nay. A long sentence is a long sentence, it's only a run-on sentence when it's not punctuated in the standard fashion. Like that one just now.

10.

The vocative comma—or the comma of direct address—is the comma separating a bit of speech from the name (or title or other identifier) of the person (or sometimes the thing) being addressed. As commas go, it's not particularly controversial. No one—at least no one I'd care to associate with—would favor

I'll meet you in the gym Charlie.

over

I'll meet you in the gym, Charlie.

Right?
And so it goes with "Good afternoon, Mabel," "I live to obey, Your Majesty," "Please don't throw me in jail,

Your Honor," and "I'll get you, my pretty, and your little dog too."

And yet—there's always an "and yet"—you probably frequently run into the likes of

And Dad, here's another thing.

or

But Mom, you said we could go to the movies.[*]

which one invariably corrects to

And, Dad, here's another thing.

and

But, Mom, you said we could go to the movies.

Copy editors periodically run into pushback—generally accompanied by a put-out "But my rhythm!"—on that comma, but they should hold firm, and writers should get over themselves. It's just a comma, and it's a

---

[*] Not to be confused with an utterly correct "But Mom said we could go to the movies."

proper and meaningful comma, and no one's pausing in midsentence to take a walk around the block.*

This is as good a place as any, I suppose, to note that honorifics either attached to names or used in place of them should be capped,† as in the aforementioned

I live to obey, Your Majesty.

and

Please don't throw me in jail, Your Honor.

Similarly, when one is speaking to one's mother or father:

I live to obey, Mom.

and

Please don't throw me in jail, Dad.

---

* The government may be reading your emails and texts, but I'm not. If you prefer "Hi John" to "Hi, John," you go right ahead.
† This does not apply to generic references to someone being addressed as "mister," "miss," "sir," or "ma'am," neither does it apply to terms of endearment like "sweetheart," "darling," "cupcake," or "honey" (unless the honey's name is Honey).

But: A passing casual reference, not in direct address, to one's mom or dad does not require a capital letter.

A bit of copyeditorial controversy tends to pop up when a writer offers something like:

I'm on my way to visit my Aunt Phyllis.

Which many copy editors will attempt to downgrade to:

I'm on my way to visit my aunt Phyllis.

Writers tend to balk at this sort of thing, and I tend to side with them. I myself had an aunt named Phyllis, and so far as I was concerned, her name was Aunt Phyllis. And thus I refer to her, always, as my Aunt Phyllis.[*]

On the other hand, I'd be more than happy to refer to "my grandmother Maude," because that is who she was, not what she was called.[†]

Note, by the way, that I do not refer to "my grandmother, Maude," since I had two grandmothers—like everyone else, whether you knew them or not. Though I

[*]   A biographer would refer to, say, "Henry VIII's aunt Mary Tudor," presuming that Henry was not in the habit of cozily addressing her as "Aunt Mary Tudor."
[†] She was called Nana, if you must know.

might well refer to "my maternal grandmother, Maude."
(See "The 'Only' Comma," in Section 13, below.)

11.

We've all been taught to precede or follow dialogue with
a comma in constructions like

> Atticus said dryly, "Do not let this inspire you to
> further glory, Jeremy."

or

> "Keep your temper," said the Caterpillar.

It should be noted, though, that this rule does not
apply when dialogue is preceded or followed by some
version of the verb "to be" ("is," "are," "was," "were,"
etc.), as in:

> Lloyd's last words were "That tiger looks highly
> pettable."

or

> "Happy New Year" is a thing you should stop
> saying after January 8.

In each of these cases, the phrase in question is less dialogue than a noun-in-quote-marks, and thus no comma is called for. If you can replace the words in quotes with "it" or "that" or another pronoun, you don't need a comma before them.

12.

Will you go to London too?
Will you go to London, too?

Q. When do I use a comma with "too" and when don't I?

A. Whichever you choose, the other way will look better.

I spent a great many years periodically revisiting my big fat stylebooks in an attempt to get it into my head how to properly do the "too" thing, and the explanations never sank in. In the examples above, does one of them mean "Will you go to London as well as Paris?" and does one of them mean "Will you as well as your mother go to London?" I haven't the foggiest. So to blazes with it. If you can hear a comma before the "too," feel free to use it. If you can't, feel free to not.

13.

THE "ONLY" COMMA

If a writer writes a sentence like

He traveled to Pompeii with his daughter Clara.

a copy editor will usually ask:

His only daughter? If so, add comma.

Thus the comma I choose to refer to—since I am perpetually confused by the grammar terms "restrictive" and "nonrestrictive" and can never remember which is meant to be which—as the "only" comma.

"Only" commas (they travel in pairs, except at the very ends of sentences), are used to set off nouns that are the only one of their kind in the vicinity, as in, say,

Abraham Lincoln's eldest son, Robert, was born on August 1, 1843.

The logic being that as one can have only one eldest son, his name in this sentence is an interesting, noteworthy, yet *inessential* piece of information. Thus if I encounter

> Abraham Lincoln's eldest son was born on
> August 1, 1843.

there can be no question that it's Robert who is being spoken of, rather than the subsequent Edward or Willie or Tad, whether Robert is named or not.

Conversely, in a sentence lacking the unique modifier "eldest," one must be told which son is being spoken of, thus:

> Lincoln's son Robert was an eyewitness to the
> assassination of President Garfield.

Or, say:

> George Saunders's book *Lincoln in the Bardo*
> concerns the death of Abraham Lincoln's son
> Willie.

Again, it's crucial, not merely interesting, that we know which of Abraham Lincoln's sons is being spoken of, and that the son in question is not Robert, Edward, or Tad.

At the other end of the spectrum, then, be careful not to set an "only" comma where there is no only-ness, as in, say:

> The Pulitzer Prize–winning novelist, Edith
> Wharton, was born in New York City.

Because Wharton is merely one of many winners of the Pulitzer, *there should be no "only" comma.*

14.

The "only" comma rule is also helpful in differentiating between "that" and "which," if differentiating between "that" and "which" is your bag.

If you're about to offer a piece of information that's crucial to your sentence, offer it up without a comma and with a "that":

> Please fetch me the Bible that's on the table.

Which is to say: Fetch me the Bible that is on the table rather than the Bible that's under the couch or the Bible that's poised picturesquely on the window seat.

If you're offering a piece of information that's perhaps interesting amplification but might well be deleted without harm, offer it up with a comma and a "which":

> Please fetch me the Bible, which is on the table.

One Bible and one Bible only.

The "that" versus "which" rule is not universally observed, I must note. Some writers find it pushily constricting and choose between the two by ear. I find it helpful and apply it consistently.

15.

What goes up must come down, and that which begins with a comma, if it is an interruption, must also end with one, as in:

> Queen Victoria, who by the end of her reign
> ruled over a good fifth of the world's
> population, was the longest-reigning monarch
> in British history till Elizabeth II surpassed her
> record in 2015.

It's that comma after "population" I want you to keep an eye on, because it has a tendency to get forgotten in sentences in which a parenthetical has been stuffed, turducken-like, into the interrupting bit, as in:

> Queen Victoria, who by the end of her reign ruled
> over a good fifth of the world's population
> (not all of whom were her own relatives,
> though it often seemed that way), was the

longest-reigning monarch in British history till Elizabeth II surpassed her record in 2015.

Colons

16.

Colons say: Here comes something! Think of colons as little trumpet blasts, attention-getting and ear-catching. They add drama.

Consider these examples, from Jennifer Longo's *What I Carry:*

> Alone in the loud dark, I knew: there was no way
> I could survive staying still, all by myself, for
> an entire year.

> "I've had these dishes in storage for years.
> Figured it was safe to bring them out: you
> don't strike me as a plate thrower."

A colon can also connect two sentences when the second amplifies or clarifies the first.

> His outfit made me dizzy: his pants were red
> plaid, his shirt was purple paisley, and his tie
> was striped yellow and green.

But colons can also be obnoxious, a little like that guy who stands up in the middle of a movie to shout and wave his arms at his friends. So don't use so many of them that you give your reader a headache.*

Apostrophes

18.

Before we get to what you do use apostrophes for, let's recount what you don't use them for.

Step back, I'm about to hit the CAPS LOCK key.

DO NOT EVER ATTEMPT TO USE AN APOSTROPHE TO PLURALIZE A WORD.

"NOT EVER" AS IN "NEVER."

Directing their disapproval toward miswritten produce signs advertising "banana's" and "potato's" (or "potatoe's" or even "potato'es"), the Brits have dubbed such incorrectly wielded squiggles "greengrocer's apostrophes." In America, where we don't have greengrocers, we should call them something else. The term I was first

---

* You'll note that Jennifer Longo lowercases the first word of a complete sentence following a colon, and that's her choice (and the choice of a lot of writers). Just between you and me, I think that capitalizing the first word (the first letter of the first word, that is) of a complete sentence after a colon gives the reader a valuable clue as to how to read on. But we can all agree that a sentence fragment, a list, etc., after a colon should begin with a lowercase letter.

taught was "idiot apostrophe," but that's not really nice, is it.

Let's simply call them errant apostrophes. Which is kind of classy, don't you think?

19.

The pluralization of abbreviations, too, requires no apostrophes. More than one IM = IMs. More than one ID = IDs. More than one ATM = ATMs. Etc.

20.

To say nothing of dos and don'ts, yeses and nos, etc.[*]

21.

There's no such word as "their's." Or "your's." We'll cover their/there/they're and your/you're later. Twice. Because the differences are crucial for anyone who wants to look even remotely educated.

22.

Here comes a major "on the other hand," though: *Do* use an apostrophe to pluralize a letter.

Mind your p's and q's.
Dot your *i*'s and cross your *t*'s.

---

[*] Some people, finding "nos" as the plural of "no" to be unsightly, opt for "noes." Which is no beauty contest winner either.

You bring home on your report card four B's and
two C's.*

23.

I'll wager you're adept at the use of apostrophes for simple possessives:

> the dog's toy
> Beyoncé's umpteenth Grammy

As to common—that is, not proper—nouns ending
with an *s,* you don't, at least not in recently published
text, encounter the likes of

> the boss' office
> the princess' tiara

which I find positively spooky-looking, and so for most
of us,

> the boss's office
> the princess's tiara

is the no-brainer way to go.

---

* Some favor omitting the apostrophe when pluralizing capital letters,
but I can't say I care for the sight of As for more than one A or Us for
more than one U. For, I'd say, obvious reasons.

Trouble knocks at the door, though, when terminal *s*'s occur at the ends of proper nouns. When the talk turns to, say, the writer of *Great Expectations,* how do we style his ownership?

Well, I can certainly tell you how *I* style it:

Charles Dickens's novels

Though you may come across a lot of discussion elsewhere about adding or not adding that *s* after the apostrophe based on pronunciation, convention, or what day of the week it is, you'll save yourself a lot of time by not thinking about these *s*'s and just applying them.

24.

The Possessivization of Martin Luther King, Jr.

Imagine if you will this headline:

MARTIN LUTHER KING, JR.,'S SPEECH MAKES
HISTORY

Let me say this about that:

That's not how this works. That's not how any of this works.

As a younger, more forward-thinking person, you

may already render the names of photocopied offspring without commas, thus:

Martin Luther King Jr.

In which case you've got it easy:

Martin Luther King Jr. was a hero of the civil
rights movement.

and thus:

Martin Luther King Jr.'s gift for oratory

Old-school construction, though, sets off a "Jr."[*]
with commas, as in:

Martin Luther King, Jr., was a masterful orator.

When possessivizing such a person, your options are

- that horror noted above, which I'll refrain
from repeating

---

[*] And, for that matter, a "Sr.," though in truth there's no reason for the
original owner of a name, whether he's replicated or not (and it's almost
always a he; there are precious few female Sr./Jr. combos), to set himself
off as "Sr." He got there first; it's his name.

- Martin Luther King, Jr.'s gift (which is admittedly a little unbalanced)
- Martin Luther King, Jr.'s, gift (better balanced, and at least not eye-stabbingly ugly)

You choose.*

25.

Let's move on to plural proper noun possessives, over which many tears have been shed, particularly around Christmas-card time.

First we have to properly construct the plurals themselves. So then:

Harry S. and Bess Truman = the Trumans
John F. and Jacqueline Kennedy = the Kennedys[†]
Barack H. and Michelle Obama = the Obamas

And, lurching backward to the birth of our republic:

John and Abigail Adams = the Adamses

---

* Psst. Take the middle option.
† People do occasionally trip over the pluralization of y-ending proper nouns, overextending the usual jelly/jellies, kitty/kitties formula. Nonetheless, JFK and Jackie were not "the Kennedies."

The pluralization of s-ending proper nouns seems to trip up a lot of people, but John and Abigail are the Adamses, as are John Quincy and Louisa, as are Rutherford B. and Lucy the Hayeses, and that seems to be that for s-ending presidents, but you get the point.

People who are perfectly content to keep up with the Joneses—and I'll wager the Joneses are good and tired of receiving Christmas cards addressed to "the Jones's"—sometimes balk at the sight of the Adamses, the Hayeses, the Reynoldses, the Dickenses, and the rest, but balk all you like, that's how the game is played.*

As to the possessives, then, a relative piece of cake:

the Trumans' singing daughter
the Adamses' celebrated correspondence
the Dickenses' train wreck of a marriage

26.

If Jeanette has some pencils and Nelson has some pencils and Jeanette and Nelson are not sharing their pencils, those pencils are:

---

* This foolproof system doesn't, alas, easily or attractively carry over to non-English s-ending names. Even I wouldn't address René and his wife, had he had one and had they been on my Christmas-card list, as "the Descarteses."

Jeanette's and Nelson's pencils

If Jeanette and Nelson co-own some pencils, they are:

Jeanette and Nelson's pencils.

27.

Q. Is it "farmer's market" or "farmers' market" or "farmers market"?

A. I'm presuming there's more than one farmer, so out goes "farmer's market."

As to the other two, is it a market belonging to farmers or a market made up of farmers?

I say the latter, so:

farmers market*

28.

Though it has its champions, the style decision to skip a title's *The* in a possessive construction, as in:

Suzanne Collins's *Hunger Games*

---

* Let's hold to "ladies' room," though, if only for parity with "men's room."

will always make me wrinkle my nose, and it can lead to such eyebrow raisers as

Jeanne Birdsall's *Penderwicks*

which looks to me like either a mild expletive or an obscure variation of Pick-Up Sticks.

Semicolons

29.

I love semicolons like I love pizza; fried pork dumplings; Venice, Italy; and the music of Ariana Grande.

Why does the sentence above include semicolons?

Because the most basic use of semicolons is to divide the items in a list any of whose individual elements mandate a comma—in this case, Venice, Italy.

Now, I might certainly have avoided semicolons by reordering the elements in the list:

I love semicolons like I love pizza, fried pork dumplings, the music of Ariana Grande, and Venice, Italy.

But semicolons are unavoidable when you must write something like:

Lucy's favorite novels are *Are You There God? It's Me, Margaret.;** *Goodbye, Mr. Terupt;* and *Hey, Kiddo.*

Because:

Lucy's favorite novels are *Are You There God? It's Me, Margaret., Goodbye, Mr. Terupt,* and *Hey, Kiddo.*

Well, how many novels is that, anyway? Three? Five?

But if that were the only use we had for semicolons, they wouldn't make so many people—lots of them writers who should know better—cringe. For some reason, those people think semicolons are show-offy.

I'll let author Lewis Thomas explain why those people are wrong:

---

* One might expect to see a comma in that title, between "There" and "God," and given the chance, I'd set one, but the redoubtable Judy Blume chose not to set a comma, and what the redoubtable Judy Blume has done, no one should think to undo.

The things I like best in T. S. Eliot's poetry, especially in the Four Quartets, are the semicolons. You cannot hear them, but they are there, laying out the connections between the images and the ideas. Sometimes you get a glimpse of a semicolon coming, a few lines farther on, and it is like climbing a steep path through woods and seeing a wooden bench just at a bend in the road ahead, a place where you can expect to sit for a moment, catching your breath.

You may not have read or even heard of T. S. Eliot (and almost certainly have not heard of Lewis Thomas), but doesn't this passage give you a sense of how evocative semicolons can be? Why limit your powers of expression by denying yourself such a precise tool? Use all the tools.

I've been known to insist that the only thing one needs to say in defense of semicolons is that the writer Shirley Jackson liked them. In support of that, I've also been known to whip out this, the opening paragraph of Jackson's masterwork *The Haunting of Hill House:*

No live organism can continue for long
to exist sanely under conditions of absolute

reality; even larks and katydids are supposed, by some, to dream. Hill House, not sane, stood by itself against its hills, holding darkness within; it had stood so for eighty years and might stand for eighty more. Within, walls continued upright, bricks met neatly, floors were firm, and doors were sensibly shut; silence lay steadily against the wood and stone of Hill House, and whatever walked there, walked alone.

One paragraph, three semicolons. Shirley Jackson might have chosen to replace those semicolons with periods and start each following clause anew, as an independent sentence. The result, though, would have been the untying, the disconnection, of these tightly woven, almost claustrophobic ideas, and instead of a paragraph that grabs you by the hand and marches you from beginning to end, you would have a collection of plain old sentences.

While we're here, I'd also like to celebrate that paragraph's final comma, perhaps my favorite piece of punctuation in all of literature. You might argue that it's unnecessary—even grammatically uncalled-for—but there it is, the last breath of the paragraph, the author's way of saying, "This is your last chance to set this book down and go do something else. Because from this point on it's just you, and me, and whatever it is that walks, and walks alone, in Hill House."

I dare you to walk away.

Parentheses

30.

A midsentence parenthetical aside (like this one) begins with a lowercase letter and ends (unless it's a question or even an exclamation!) without terminal punctuation.

When a fragmentary parenthetical aside comes at the very end of a sentence, make sure that the period stays outside the aside (as here).

(Only a freestanding parenthetical aside, like this one, begins with a capital letter and concludes with an appropriate bit of terminal punctuation inside the final parenthesis.)

31.

This is correct:

> Remind me again why I care what this social nobody (and her boring boyfriend) think about anything.

This is not correct:

> Remind me again why I care what this social
> nobody (and her boring boyfriend) thinks
> about anything.

An "and" is an "and," and the use of parentheses (or commas or dashes) to break up a plural subject for whatever reason does not negate the pluralness of the subject. Now, if instead of writing "and," I'd written "to say nothing of," "as well as," or "not to mention," then I'd have made me a singular subject:

> Remind me again why I care what this social
> nobody (to say nothing of her boring
> boyfriend) thinks about anything.

Brackets

32.

Brackets—or square brackets, as they're called by people who call parentheses round brackets—serve a limited but crucial purpose.

First: If you find yourself making a parenthetical comment within a parenthetical comment, the enclosed parenthetical comment is set within brackets. But it's extraordinarily unattractive on the page (I try to find a way around it [I mean, truly, do you like the way this looks?], at least whenever I can), so avoid it.

Second: Anytime you find yourself sticking a bit of your own text into quoted material (a helpfully added clarifying first name, for instance, when the original text contained only a surname) or in any other way altering a quotation, you must—and I mean must—enclose your added words in brackets.

Ah, yes, there's an exception, as there always is: If in the context of what you're writing you need to change, in quoted material, a capital letter at the beginning of a sentence to a lowercase one, or vice versa, you may do that without brackets.

That is, if you're quoting Lin-Manuel Miranda's "Wait for It" from *Hamilton,* which says "Love doesn't discriminate / Between the sinners / And the saints / It takes and it takes and it takes / And we keep loving anyway," you're well within your rights to refer to Miranda's assertion that "love doesn't discriminate" rather than his assertion that "[l]ove doesn't discriminate."

And in the other direction, quoting Miranda from *In the Heights,* "Reports of my fame are greatly exaggerated / Exacerbated by the fact that my syntax is highly complicated 'cause / I emigrated from the single greatest little place in the Caribbean," you're allowed to do this:

"My syntax is highly complicated," Miranda's character comments.

Rather than this:

"[M]y syntax is highly complicated," Miranda's character comments.

33.

[*Sic*] Burns

Let's take a moment to talk about [*sic*]. *Sic* is Latin for "thus," and it's used—traditionally in italics, always in brackets—in quoted material to make it clear to the reader that a misspelling or eccentricity or error of fact came from the person you're quoting, not from you. As, for instance and strictly speaking, you might do here, in quoting this piece of text I 100 percent made up out of thin air and didn't find on, say, Twitter:

Their [*sic*] was no Collusion [*sic*] and there was no Obstruction [*sic*].

Essentially you're saying yes, I know this is wrong, but that's how it was written, so it's not my fault.

But seriously now:

If you're quoting a lot of, say, seventeenth-century writing in which there are numerous old-fashioned-isms you wish to retain, you'd do well, somewhere around the beginning of what you're writing, perhaps in an author's note or a footnote, to make it clear that you're quoting your venerable material verbatim. That'll save you a lot of [*sic*]ing, though you might occasionally drop in a [*sic*] for an error or peculiarity whose misreading or misinterpretation might truly be confusing to your reader.

Writers of nonfiction occasionally choose, when they're quoting a good deal of archaic or otherwise peculiar material, to silently correct outdated spellings or misspellings, irregular capitalization, unusual or missing punctuation, etc.—that is, to simply impose modern spelling and grammar rules without telling the reader they're doing it. I'm not a huge fan of this practice—mostly because I think it's not as much fun as retaining all that flavorful weirdness—though I can understand why you might do it in a work of nonfiction that's meant to be popular rather than scholarly. If you're going to do it, again, let the reader know up front. It's only fair.

Do not—not as in never—use [*sic*] as a snide comment to suggest that something you're quoting is dopey. By which I mean the very meaning of the words, not merely their spelling. You may think you're getting in a good shot at a writer whose judgment you find shaky; the only person whose judgment is going to seem shaky is you.

It's the prose equivalent of using scare quotes (see page 62) or wearing an I'M WITH STUPID T-shirt, and just about as charming.

Quotation Marks

When I was growing up in Albertson, Long Island, a virtually undetectable suburb of New York City, my mother would regularly send me off on my bike to the nearby bakery for a rye bread (sliced) or a challah (unsliced) or six rolls.

In the bakery, above the rye bread, was a sign that read:

TRY OUR RUGELACH! IT'S THE "BEST!"

I was fascinated. This, as they say in the comic books, is my origin story.

So, then, to break it down for you:

34.

Use roman (straight up and down, that is, like the font this phrase is printed in) type encased in quotation marks for the titles of songs, poems, short stories, and episodes of TV series. Whereas the titles of music albums, volumes of poetry, full-length works of fiction and nonfiction, and TV series themselves are styled in aslant italics.

"American Idiot"
American Idiot

"Song of Myself"
Leaves of Grass

"The Lottery"
The Lottery and Other Stories

"Lies My Parents Told Me"
Buffy the Vampire Slayer (also known as, simply, *Buffy*)

It's a fairly simple system: little things in roman and quotes, bigger things in italics.

35.

Individual works of art—named paintings and sculptures—are generally set in italics (*The Luncheon* on the Grass), though works whose titles are unofficial (the Winged Victory of Samothrace and the Mona Lisa, for instance) are often styled in roman, without quotation marks.

36.

Dialogue is set off with quotation marks. Some writers like to do without them, to which I simply say: To pull that off, you have to be awfully good at differentiating between narration and dialogue. It's a sophisticated style choice.

37.

Once upon a time, what I'd call articulated rumination (a direct, dialogue-like thought not expressed aloud) was often found encased in quotation marks:

"What is to become of me?" Estelle thought.

That, over time, gave way to setting direct thoughts in italics:

What is to become of me? Estelle thought.

Now, more often than not, you'll simply see:

What is to become of me? Estelle thought.

That last is best.[*]

38.

Do not use quotation marks for emphasis—as in, for instance:

> Last week we went to the Jersey Shore, and I had the "best" time.

That is why we invented italics.

Such quotation marks do not, strictly speaking, come under the heading of scare quotes, which are quotation marks used to convey that you find a term too slangish or dorky or ridiculous to sit on its own and/or are sneering at it:

> That "music" you're listening to is . . . interesting.

Avoid scare quotes. They'll make you look snotty.

---

[*] Six consecutive words set in italics aren't going to bother anyone, but I caution you against setting anything longer than a single sentence that way. For one thing, italics weary the eye; for another, multiple paragraphs of text set in italics suggest a dream sequence, and everyone skips dream sequences.

39.

Do not use quotation marks after the term "so-called." For instance, I'm not

a so-called "expert" in matters copyeditorial

I'm simply a

so-called expert in matters copyeditorial

The quotation-marking of something following "so-called" is not only redundant but makes a likely already judgmental sentence even more so.

40.

In referring to a word or words as a word or words, some people go with quotation marks and some people prefer italics, as in:

The phrase "the fact that" is to be avoided.

or

The phrase *the fact that* is to be avoided.

The first example is chattier, I think, more like speech; the second is more technical- and textbooky-looking. Either one is fine. It's a matter of taste.

41.

An exclamation point or question mark at the end of a sentence ending with a bit of quoted matter goes outside rather than inside the quotation marks if the exclamation point or question mark belongs to the larger sentence rather than to the quoted bit, as in:

> As you are not dear to me and we are not friends, please don't ever refer to me as "my dear friend"!

What happens when both the quoted material and the surrounding sentence demand emphatic or inquiring punctuation? Do you really write

> You'll be sorry if you ever again say to me, "But you most emphatically are my dear friend!"!

No, you do not. You make a choice as to where the ! might be more effective. (In the example above, I'd keep the first exclamation point.) Or you rewrite your sentence to avoid the collision entirely.

42.

In American English, we reach first for double quotation marks, as I've been doing all this time. If you need to quote something within quotation marks, you use single quotation marks. As in:

> "I was quite surprised," Jeannine commented, "when Mabel said to me, 'I'm leaving tomorrow for Chicago,' then walked out the door."

If you find yourself with yet another layer of quoted material, you then revert to double quotation marks, like this:

> "I was quite surprised," Jeannine commented, "when Mabel said to me, 'I've found myself lately listening over and over to the song "Baby Shark,"' then proceeded to sing it."

Do, though, try to avoid this Russian doll punctuation; it's hard on the eye and on the brain.

Moreover, I caution you generally, re quotes within quotes: It's easy to lose track of what you're doing and set double quotes within double quotes. Be on your guard.

43.

Though semicolons, because they are elusive and enigmatic and they like it that way, are set outside terminal quotation marks, periods and commas—and if I make this point once, I'll make it a thousand times, and trust me, I will—are always set inside.

Always.

Hyphens

44.

If you turn to page 719 in your *Merriam-Webster's Collegiate Dictionary,* eleventh edition, you will find, one atop the other:

light-headed
lighthearted

Which tells you pretty much everything you want to know about the use of hyphens, which is to say: It doesn't make much sense, does it.

If you type "lightheaded" (I note that my spellcheck dots have not popped up) or "light-hearted," the hyphen police are surely not going to come after you, and I won't even notice, but:

If you're invested in getting your hyphens correctly sorted out in compound adjectives, verbs, and nouns, and you like being told what to do, just pick up your dictionary and look 'em up. Those listings are *correct.*

45.

That said, you will find—if you've a penchant for noticing these things—that compounds have a tendency, over time, to spit out unnecessary hyphens and close themselves up. Over the course of my career I've seen "light bulb" evolve into "light-bulb" and then into "lightbulb," "baby-sit" give way to "babysit," and—a big one—"Web site" turn into "Web-site," then, happily, "website."

46.

However, convention (aka tradition, aka consensus, aka it's simply how it's done, so don't argue with it) allows for exceptions in some cases in which a misreading is unlikely, as in, say:

> real estate agent
> high school students

Generally—yes, exceptions apart, there are always exceptions—you use a hyphen or hyphens in these before-the-noun (there goes another one) adjectival cases to avoid that momentary unnecessary hesitation we're always trying to spare our readers.

Consider the difference between, say, "a man eating

shark" and "a man-eating shark," where the hyphen is crucial in clarifying who is eating whom, and "a cat related drama," which could mean that a cat told a riveting story, and "a cat-related drama," which is what you meant in the first place.

So as we navigate these migraine-inducing points of trivia, impossible-to-understand differentiations, and inconsistently applied rules, do you wonder why, though I hyphenated "migraine-inducing" and "impossible-to-understand," I left "inconsistently applied" open?

Because compounds formed from an "-ly" adverb and an adjective or participle do not take a hyphen:

inconsistently applied rules
maddeningly irregular punctuation
beautifully arranged sentences

Why?

Because the possibility of misreading is slim to nil, so a hyphen is unnecessary.

Or, if you prefer a simpler explanation:

Because.*

---

* Footnote pop quiz: So why would I hyphenate the likes of "scholarly-looking teenagers" or "lovely-smelling flowers"? Because not all "-ly" words are adverbs. Sometimes they're adjectives. Really, I'm sorry.

47.

Modern style is to merge prefixes and main words (nouns, verbs, adjectives) seamlessly and hyphenlessly, as in:

antiwar
autocorrect
codependent
extracurricular
hyperactive
interdepartmental
nonnative
outfight
reelect
subpar

I'd suggest that you follow this streamlined style.

But: If you find any given hyphenated compound incomprehensible or too hideous to stand (antiinflammatory, antieducational), it's OK to hold on to that hyphen. Remember, your goal is to make yourself understood. And the dictionary can help out when you just can't decide.

48.

There are some exceptions.

Aren't there always?

To recreate is to enjoy recreation, but to create

something anew is to re-create it. And you may reform a naughty child, but if you are taking that child literally apart and putting it back together, you are re-forming it. You may quit your after-school job by resigning, but a contract, once signed, can certainly be re-signed.

49.

The age of people's children trips up a lot of people with children.

> My daughter is six years old.
> My six-year-old daughter is off to summer camp.
> My daughter, a six-year-old, is off to summer
>   camp.

You'll often encounter "a six-year old girl" or, though it would be correct only in a discussion of sextuplets who have just celebrated their first birthday, "six year-olds." Please get it right.

Dashes

50.

Dashes come in two flavors: em and en. Em dashes (which most people simply refer to as dashes) are so called because they were traditionally the width of a capital *M* in any particular typeface (nowadays they tend to be a touch wider); en dashes are the width of a lowercase *n*.

This is an em dash: —

This, just a touch shorter yet still longer than a hyphen, is an en dash: –

Likely you don't need much advice from me on how to use em dashes, because you all seem to use an awful lot of them.

They're useful for interruption of dialogue, either midsentence from within:

> "Once upon a time—yes, I know you've heard
> this story before—there lived a princess
> named Snow White."

or to convey interruption from without:

> "The murderer," she intoned, "is someone in
> this—"
> A shot rang out.

And they nicely set off a bit of text in standard narration when commas—because that bit of text is rather on the parenthetical side, like this one, but you don't want to use parentheses—won't do the trick:

He packed his bag with all the things he thought
he'd need for the weekend—an array of
T-shirts, two pairs of socks per day, all the
clean underwear he could locate—and made
his way to the airport.

According to copyediting tradition—at least copyediting tradition as it was handed down to me—you should
use no more than two em dashes in a single sentence, and I
think that's good advice—except when it's not.

En dashes are the guild secret of copyediting, and
most normal people neither use them nor much know
what they are nor even know how to type them.[*] I'm
happy to reveal the secret.

An en dash is used to hold words together instead of
your standard hyphen, which usually does the trick just
fine, when you're connecting a multiword proper noun to
another multiword proper noun or to pretty much anything else. What the heck does that mean? It means this:

a Lana Condor–Noah Centineo romance
a New York–to–Chicago flight

---

[*] On a Mac, you can create an en dash by typing option-hyphen. On
an iPhone, if you lean gently on the hyphen key, an en dash will present
itself, as well as an em dash and a bullet. On a PC, I believe you type
command–3 and say "Abracadabra!"

a World War II–era plane
a Pulitzer Prize–winning play

Basically, that which you're connecting needs a smidgen more connecting than can be accomplished with a hyphen.

Please note in the second example above that I've used two en dashes rather than an en dash and a hyphen, even though "Chicago" is a single word. Why? Visual balance, that's all. This

a New York–to-Chicago flight

simply looks—to me and now, I hope, to you, forever afterward—lopsided.

I've also seen attempted, in an attempt to style the last example, the use of multiple hyphens, as in:

a Pulitzer-Prize-winning play

That simply doesn't look very nice, does it?

You don't want to make en dashes do too much heavy lifting, though. They work well visually, but they have their limits as far as meaning is concerned. The likes of

the ex–prime minister

certainly makes sense and follows the rules, but

the former prime minister

works just as well.
And something like

an anti–air pollution committee

would be better as

an anti-air-pollution committee

or perhaps should be rethought altogether.
En dashes are also used for

page references (pp. 3–21)
sporting game scores (the Yankees clobbered the
    Mets, 14–2)[*]
court decisions (the Supreme Court upheld the
    lower court's ruling by a 7–2 vote)

---

[*] I'd originally written "the Mets clobbered the Yankees," but a friend, reading the text, insisted I switch the teams "FOR REALISM." Shows you how much I know about (no, I'm not going to write "football," because some jokes are too easy, even for me) baseball.

Question Marks and Exclamation Points

51.

If a sentence is constructed like a question but isn't intended to be one, you might consider concluding it with a period rather than a question mark. "That's a good idea, don't you think?" means something quite different from "That's a horrible idea, isn't it."

52.

Go light on the exclamation points. When overused, they're bossy, alarming, and, ultimately, wearying. Some writers say you should use no more than a dozen exclamation points per book; others insist that you should use no more than a dozen exclamation points in a lifetime.

53.

That said, it would be irresponsible not to properly convey with an exclamation mark the excitement of something like "Your hair is on fire!" The person with the burning head might not believe you otherwise. And "What a lovely day!" with a period rather than a bang, as some people like to call the exclamation point, might seem sarcastic. Or depressed.

54.

If you're not writing a comic book, you shouldn't end any sentence with a double exclamation point or double question mark. You might want to tell your teacher exactly how much you hated the book you're writing your report on, but do it without getting overexcited.

55.

Sentences beginning with "I wonder" are not questions—they're simply pondering declarations—and do not conclude with question marks.

I wonder who's hacking the school website.
I wonder what the king is doing tonight.

56.

Neither are sentences beginning with "Guess who" or "Guess what" questions. If anything, they're imperatives.

Guess who's coming to dinner.

CHAPTER 3

1, 2, 3, GO

The Treatment of Numbers

Generally, write out numbers from one through one hundred and all numbers beyond that are easily expressed in words—that is, two hundred but 250, eighteen hundred but 1,823. Print periodicals with a desire to conserve space often set the writing-out limit at "nine" or "ten," but if you've got all the room in the world, words are, I'd say, friendlier-looking on the page.

1.

If in any given paragraph (or, to some eyes, on any given page) one particular number mandates the use of numerals, then all *related* uses of numbers should also be styled in numerals. That is, not:

> The farmer lived on seventy-five fertile acres and
> owned twelve cows, thirty-seven mules, and
> 126 chickens.

but rather:

> The farmer lived on seventy-five fertile acres and
> owned 12 cows, 37 mules, and 126 chickens.

2.

Numerals are generally avoided in dialogue. That is:

> "I bought sixteen apples, eight bottles of
> sparkling water, and thirty-two cans of soup,"
> said James, improbably.

rather than

> "I bought 16 apples, 8 bottles of sparkling water,
> and 32 cans of soup," said James, improbably.

But don't take your avoidance of numerals to extremes. You certainly don't want anything that looks even vaguely like this:

> "And then, in nineteen eighty-three," Dave
> recounted, "I drove down Route Sixty-Six,
> pulled in to a Motel Six, and stayed overnight
> in room four-oh-two, all for the low, low price

of seventeen dollars and seventy-five cents, including tax."

2a.

Should a character say "I arrived at four thirty-two" or "I arrived at 4:32"?

Unless you are forensically reconstructing the time-line of a series of unsolved murders, a character should, please, simply say "I arrived just after four-thirty."

And a character might well say "I left at 4:45," and I think that looks just dandy ("I left at four forty-five," if you absolutely must), but a character might also say "I left at a quarter to five."

3.

It's considered bad form to begin a sentence with a numeral or numerals.

> NO: 1967 dawned clear and bright.
>
> BETTER, THOUGH NOT GREAT: Nineteen sixty-seven dawned clear and bright.
>
> BETTER STILL, ALBEIT TAUTOLOGICAL: The year 1967 dawned clear and bright.
>
> EVEN BETTER: Recast your sentence so it doesn't begin with a year.

4.

When writing of time, I favor, for example:

> five A.M.
> 4:32 P.M.

using those pony-size capital letters (affectionately known as small caps*) rather than the horsier A.M./P.M. or the desultory-looking a.m./p.m. (AM/PM and am/pm are out of the question.)

By the way, the likes of "6 A.M. in the morning" is a redundancy that turns up with great frequency, so I warn you against it. It's 6 A.M. or six in the morning. You don't need both.

5.

For years, then:

> 53 B.C.
> A.D. 1654

---

* In Microsoft Word you can create small caps by either typing the letters in question in lowercase, highlighting them, then hitting Command+Shift+K or, if that's not a thing you can readily remember, typing the letters in question in lowercase, highlighting them, then heading up to the top of your screen and fiddling your way through Format and Font.

You will note, please, that B.C. ("before Christ," as I likely don't have to remind you) is always set after the year and A.D. (the Latin *anno Domini,* meaning "in the year of the Lord") before it.

Perhaps you were taught to use the non-Jesus-oriented B.C.E. (before the Common Era) and C.E. (of the Common Era). If so, note that both B.C.E. and C.E. are set after the year:

53 B.C.E.
1654 C.E.

I'll note that, at least in my experience, writers still overwhelmingly favor B.C. and A.D., and that B.C.E. and C.E. remain about as popular, at least in the United States, as the metric system.

Just, please, make sure you get everything in the right place. Should I ever be touring the Moon,* you can be certain that my first order of business will be to take a Sharpie to the plaque that refers to humanity's arrival there in "JULY 1969, A. D."†

---

* You may well encounter contradicting style advice on Moon/moon (speaking of our particular one, that is), Sun/sun (ditto), and Earth/earth (the planet, not the dirt thereon). Let your context be your guide.
† There are a few other things wrong with that plaque, but that's a conversation for another day.

6.

I refer to the years from 1960 to 1969[*] as the sixties (or, in a pinch, as the '60s) and the streets of Manhattan from Sixtieth through Sixty-ninth as the Sixties. Some people do it the other way around, but let's not fight about it.

Or let's. I win.

7.

If you're writing dates U.S.-style, note the invariable commas on either side of the year, as in:

> Emma Stone was born on November 6, 1988, in
> Scottsdale, Arizona.

If you're writing dates the way people just about anywhere else in the world write them, you can save up your commas for some other use:

> Emma Stone was born on 6 November 1988 in
> Scottsdale, Arizona.

Note as well that even if your mind may be hearing "November sixth," you don't, in just about any con-

---

[*] Be careful not to write "the years from 1960–1969." If you've got a "from," you need a "to."

text, write "November 6th." I don't know why; you just don't.

8.

The use of 555 phone numbers looks just as silly[*] on the page as it sounds in movies or on television. A tiny amount of ingenuity dodges the problem.

> "What's your phone number?"
> I jotted it down on a scrap of paper and handed
>   it to her.

9.

Miscellaneously:

- Degrees of temperature ("a balmy 83 degrees") and longitude/latitude (38°41'7.8351", and note the use not only of the degree symbol but of those austere vertical prime marks, not to be confused with stylishly curly quotation marks) are best set in numerals.

---

[*] How easy was it not to write a sentence beginning, "555 phone numbers are just as silly-looking"? Quite.

- So are biblical references to chapter and verse (Exodus 3:12, for instance).
- Except in dialogue, percentages should be expressed as numerals, though I'd urge you to use the word "percent" rather than the percentage sign—unless what you're writing is hugely about percentages or you're doing a math assignment, in which case feel free to write "95%" rather than "95 percent" (unless you're doing your math homework).
- Particularly numbery things, like ball game scores ("The Yankees were up 11–2") and Supreme Court rulings ("the 7–2 decision in the Dred Scott case"), look best expressed in numerals. Plus they give you the chance to make good use of those excellent en dashes.

10.

A crucial, *crucial* thing about numbers, no matter how they're styled:

They need to be accurate.

As soon as you write something like "Here are twelve helpful rules for college graduates heading into the job market," alert readers start counting. You'd be surprised at how many lists of twelve things contain only eleven things. This is an easy thing to overlook, but don't. Otherwise you'll find yourself with a chapter titled "56 Assorted Things to Do (and Not to Do) with Punctuation" that contains 55 assorted things. Because I skipped number 17. Did you notice?

CHAPTER 4

A LITTLE GRAMMAR
IS A DANGEROUS THING

I'm going to let you in on a little secret:

I hate grammar.

Well, OK, not quite true. I don't hate grammar. I hate grammar jargon.

When I started out as a copy editor, I realized that most of what I knew about grammar I knew instinctively. That is, I knew how most—certainly not all—of the grammar things worked; I simply didn't know what they were called.

Even now I'd be hard-pressed to tell you what a nominative absolute is, I think that the word "genitive" sounds vaguely smutty, and I don't know, or care to know, how to diagram a sentence.

I hope I'm not shocking you.

But at a certain point I figured that if I was going to be fixing grammar for a living, I might do well to learn a little something about it, and that's precisely what I did: I learned a little something about it. As little as I needed to. I still, at the slightest puzzlement, run back to my big fat stylebooks, and likely always will.

I do believe, though, that if as a writer you know how to do a thing, it's not terribly important that you know what it's called. So in this chapter—covering the grammar stumbles I tend to run into most frequently—I'll do my best to keep the information as simple and applicable as possible and skip the terminology.

1.

Here's one of those grammar rules that infuriate people:

That's it. That's the rule, or at least an example of it: The correct verb in that sentence is not "infuriates" but "infuriate."

I know that you want to match "one" with a singular verb, but (and I'm now quoting my beloved *Words into Type*) "the verb in a relative clause [in my example, the verb "infuriate" in the relative clause "that infuriate people"] agrees with the antecedent of the relative pronoun [in my example, the antecedent is "rules"], which is the nearest noun or pronoun and is often the object of a preposition, as in the phrase *one of those who* [or] *one of the things that.*"

2.

Even as I type these words, I'm listening to a wonderful singer whom I saw onstage repeatedly and who I didn't realize had died twenty years ago.

The reports of the imminent death of the word "whom," to paraphrase that which Mark Twain never quite said,[*] are greatly exaggerated, so you'd do well to learn to use it correctly or, at least and perhaps more important, learn not to use it incorrectly.[†]

Basic "whom" use shouldn't pose too many challenges. If you can remember to think of "who" as the cousin of "I," "he," "she," and "they" (the thing doing the thing, aka a subject) and to think of "whom" as the cousin of "me," "him," "her," and "them" (the thing being done to, aka an object), you're most of the way there.

The man whom Shirley met for lunch was
wearing a green carnation in his lapel.

---

[*] What Mark Twain did say—write, in a note, to be accurate—was "James Ross Clemens, a cousin of mine, was seriously ill two or three weeks ago in London, but is well now. The report of my illness grew out of his illness; the report of my death was an exaggeration."

[†] I'm concerned with how you write, not how you speak, so if you're prone to saying "It's me" rather than "It is I" or inquiring "Who do you love?" rather than "Whom do you love?," you're A-OK tops in my book, and in the book of just about anyone else who aspires to speak English like a normal human being.

(You'll note that this sentence would work just as well if you deleted the "whom" altogether. Same goes for the sentence about the singer a handful of paragraphs north of here.)

To whom did you give the shirt off your back?

To say nothing of "to whom it may concern" and *For Whom the Bell Tolls*.

The thing to avoid is, in a moment of panic or in an attempt to prove how smart you are, using "whom" when what you really want is "who." This sort of error is generally referred to as a hypercorrection, a term I'm not enamored of and that, I've found, confuses people, because the point of a hypercorrection is not that it's superduper correct but that it's trying so hard to be correct that it collapses into error. But until someone can come up with a better word, we're stuck with it.

"Whom" hypercorrections—and "whomever" hyper-corrections, so long as we're here—tend to fall into two camps: the "No, that's a parenthetical phrase" camp and the "Watch out for that verb!" camp.

For the former, let's think of Viola, the heroine of Shakespeare's *Twelfth Night,* and her brother, Sebastian, whom she believes has drowned in a shipwreck.

No. The "she believes" is parenthetical, settable-off-with-commas, or even utterly extractable. Let's dig in:

> her brother, Sebastian, whom has drowned in a
> shipwreck

Well, that won't do, now, will it. So then:

> her brother, Sebastian, who she believes has
> drowned in a shipwreck

In this case, your hypercorrection alarm should ring over the likes of "she believes," "he says," "it is thought," etc.

Is there a correct "whom" version of that phrase? Sure, let's try this (though it's a bit of a mouthful):

> her brother, Sebastian, whom, supposedly
> drowned in a shipwreck, she mourns

The "Watch out for that verb!" hypercorrection occurs when you've got everything cued up perfectly:

> I gave the candy to

and you're so dang sure that the next word is, well, of course, an object-type thing—a "him," a "her," a "them"—that you continue

I gave the candy to whomever wanted it the most.

And no again. It's that following verb, that "wanted," that itself demands a subject, leading to a correct:

I gave the candy to whoever wanted it the most.

You can, to be sure, give the candy to whomever you like, and that will be correct too.

Your hypercorrection alarm, in this case, should sound at the sight of a new verb on the horizon, and a lot of the time that verb is going to be an "is," as in:

I will give the candy to whoever is most
    deserving.

3.

In "not x but y," "not only x but y," "either x or y," "neither x nor y," and "both x and y" constructions, you must ensure that the x and the y match in their makeup—that is to say, are parallel.

(Many people, I've found, have lodged in their heads the absolute necessity of including an "also" in this construction, not merely "not only x but y" but "not only x but also y." Seems like a waste of a good "also" to me. I *would* include an "also" if I chose to express myself thus: "Not only did I write a note to myself to write about 'not only x but y' constructions; I also wrote a note to myself to write about 'either x or y' constructions." But I don't think I'd choose to express myself thus.)

It's an easy thing to get wrong—I can assure you of that firsthand. It's quite easy to write:

> She achieved success not only through native
>   intelligence but perseverance.

and not give it a second thought. But you do want to get this correct, so:

> She achieved success not only through native
>   intelligence but through perseverance.
> She achieved success through not only native
>   intelligence but perseverance.

Similarly:

NO: I can either attempt to work all afternoon or
  I can go buy new shoes.
YES: I can either attempt to work all afternoon or
  go buy new shoes.
ALSO YES: Either I can attempt to work all
  afternoon or I can go buy new shoes.

Oh, and this:

In "neither x nor y" constructions, if the x is singular
and the y is plural, the verb to follow is plural. If the x is
plural and the y is singular, the verb to follow is singular.
That is, simply: Take your cue from the y.

Neither the president nor the representatives
  have the slightest idea what's going on.
Neither the representatives nor the president has
  the slightest idea what's going on.

4.

Q. Is it "It is I who is late" or "It is I who am late"?

A. It's "I'm late." Why make things more complicated
than they need to be?

5.

A student should be able to study what they like, right? That "they"—that distinctly singular "they"—is a grammatical flashpoint. Some people take the singular "they" in stride and think that sentence is fine as it is. Others would balk and rewrite it to, for instance, "Students should be able to study what they like," which is certainly an easy and grammatical solution. (In the old days you might have seen something like "A student should be able to study what he likes," but in the old days people wrote a lot of things that don't work anymore.)

The proscription against the singular "they," I can report, is yet another of those Victorian-era pulled-out-of-relatively-thin-air grammar rules we've been saddled with, and I'm going to assert here, perhaps to the chagrin of some older writers and/or grammarians, that it's a rule we should let go of. The singular "they" is not the wave of the future; it's the wave of the present.

That said, please don't embrace the singular "they" so vigorously that you find yourself writing things like "Every girl in the sorority should do what they like" or "A boy's best friend is their mother," because that would be quite, quite daft.

A further—and, I think, crucial—point:

When I first drafted this section, I relegated the discussion of the use of pronouns for nonbinary people—

people who do not identify as male or female—to a terse footnote acknowledging the relatively recent invention of alternate pronouns (I guess I've encountered the "ze"/"zir" system most frequently, but there are a number of others) and the increasing use of what one might call a particularly singular "they" and excused myself from discussing it.

In other words, I chickened out.

And yet: I now have a colleague whose pronoun of choice is "they," and thus the issue is no longer culturally abstract but face-to-face personal, no longer an issue I'd persuaded myself was none of my business but one of basic human respect I chose—choose—to embrace. (I'm happy to call myself out for stubbornly avoiding the topic till it became personal. We're all supposed to be better than that, but we often aren't.)

6.

Here's a sentence I was recently on the verge of making public:

> I think of the internet as a real place, as real or realer than Des Moines.

If you recognize immediately what's the matter with that sentence, you've already grasped the concept of parallelism. If you haven't—and don't be hard on yourself if you haven't, because you're in the occasional company of just about every writer I've ever encountered—here is the correct version:

> I think of the internet as a real place, as real as or
> realer than Des Moines.

It's all about that third "as." How come? "As real" and "realer than" do not match in construction, as you'll note if, in my original sentence, you flip them around:

> I think of the internet as a real place, realer than
> or as real Des Moines.

Sentences lacking parallelism are direly easy to construct. Here's another:

> A mother's responsibilities are to cook, clean,
> and the raising of the children.

Which should correctly be:

> A father's responsibilities are to cook, to clean,
> and to raise the children.

Everything's nice and matchy-matchy now.

There's something bracingly attractive about a sentence that brims with parallelism:

> He was not beholden to, responsible for, or in
> any other way interested in the rule of law.

7.

At some point in your life, perhaps now, it may occur to you that the phrase "aren't I" is a grammatical train wreck. You can, at that point, either spend the rest of your life saying "am I not?" or "amn't I?," or you can simply embrace, as you surely already have, yet another of those oddball constructions that sneak into the English language and achieve widespread acceptance, all the while giggling to themselves at having gotten away with something.

8.

> Flipping restlessly through the channels, John
> Huston's *The Treasure of the Sierra Madre*
> was playing on TCM.

Huston, we have a problem.

Improperly attaching itself to the sentence's subject—

that is, "John Huston's *The Treasure of the Sierra Madre*"—we in the copyediting business call that introductory bit (that is, "Flipping restlessly through the channels") a dangler.

This particular flavor of dangler is called in full a dangling participle, but not all danglers are participles, and anyway, using the term "dangling participle" mandates that you know what a participle is. "Dangling modifier"—sometimes one runs into the term "misattached modifier" or "misplaced modifier"—makes for a better overall designation, but "dangler" is easier and quicker, so let's just stick with that. Whatever we're calling them, danglers are, I'd say, the most common error committed in otherwise competent prose and by far the error that most often makes it to print. Authors write them, copy editors overlook them, proofreaders speed past them. It's not a good look.

Essentially, a sentence's introductory bit and its main bit need to fuse correctly. Or, as I like to think of it, they need to talk to each other. If a sentence begins "Flipping restlessly through the channels," then the sentence's subject—more than likely, its very next word—has to tell us who's holding the remote. It might be "I," it might be "he," it might be "Cecilia," but it's certainly not "John Huston's *The Treasure of the Sierra Madre*."

Strolling through the park, the weather was
beautiful. *Nope.*
The weather was beautiful as we strolled through
the park. *Yup.*

Arriving at the garage, my bike was nowhere to
be found. *Nah.*
When I arrived at the garage, my bike was
nowhere to be found. *Yeah.*

Perhaps these sorts of errors seem obvious to you—particularly since we're talking about them here and staring at them—but, as I said, they can slip right past you if you're not paying attention.

For instance, please hop back up a few paragraphs and take another look at the sentence that begins "Improperly attaching itself."

Yeah. Dangler.

I encounter danglers all the time. They frequently turn up in donated bits of praise generously provided by writers to support other writers—blurbs, that is. "An intoxicating mix of terror and romance, Olga Bracely has penned her best novel yet!"

No.

9.

A sentence whose parts are misarranged to inadvertent comic effect can be a kind of dangler, but mostly I think of it simply as a sentence whose parts are misarranged to inadvertent comic effect.

Or to advert comic effect, if you're Groucho Marx: "One morning I shot an elephant in my pajamas. How he got into my pajamas, I'll never know."

Or perhaps you've met that famous man with a wooden leg named Smith.

10.

You'd be amazed at how far you can get in life having no idea what the subjunctive mood is—as if it's not bad enough that English has rules, it also has moods—but as long as I've brought the subject up, let's address it.

The subjunctive mood is used to convey various flavors of nonreality. For instance, it dictates the use of "were" rather than "was" in Beyoncé's "If I Were a Boy."

"I wish I were" rather than "I wish I was" seems to come naturally to most people, so let's simply say amen to that and leave it be. The tricky part comes with the juxtaposition of:

"if"

"I," "he," or "she"*

"was" or "were"

Now, if you're lucky enough to be writing a sentence that includes not merely "if" but "as if," you can simply grab on to "were" and run with it:

I felt as if I were a peony in a garden of dandelions.

He comports himself as if he were the king of England.†

But when you've got only an "if" in your hands, when do you use "was" and when do you use "were"?

Try this on for size: If you're writing of a situation that is not merely not the case but is unlikely, improbable, or just plain impossible, you can certainly reach for a "were."

---

* To be sure, "you" and "we" and "they" are always matched with "were," so that's one less problem—or three less/fewer problems—to contend with.

† It's indeed "the king of England," not "the King of England." We capitalize a job title when it's used as an honorific, as in "President Barack Obama," but otherwise it's "the president of the United States," "the pope," and the various other et ceteras.

> If I were to win the lottery tomorrow, I'd quit my
> job so fast it would make your head spin.

If you're writing of a situation that is simply not the case but could be, you might opt for a *was*.

> If he was to walk into the room right now, I'd
> give him a good piece of my mind.

I tend to think of it thus: If I could insert the words "in fact" after "if I," I might well go with a "was" rather than a "were."

Also, if you're acknowledging some action or state of being that most certainly did occur—that is, if by "if" what you really mean is "in that"—you want a "was":

> If I was hesitant to embrace your suggestion
> yesterday, it was simply that I was too
> distracted to properly absorb it.

Other Dangerous Things: Foreign Affairs

Standard practice is to set foreign-language words and phrases in italics. If a word or phrase, however foreign-language-derived, is included in the main part of your handy *Merriam-Webster's Collegiate Dictionary*, eleventh edition, it's to be taken as English. If it's tucked into the appendix of foreign-language words and phrases at the back of the book (or is not to be found at all), it's to be taken as not-English.

The following, then, can be taken as English:

bête noire
carpe diem
château
chutzpah
façade
hausfrau
karaoke
mea culpa
non sequitur
schadenfreude[*]

The following can be taken as not-English:

dasvidaniya
e pluribus unum
n'est-ce pas?
und so weiter

---

[*] Nouns in German are capitalized, but I figure that if a common German noun has made its way into standard English, it should be lowercased like any other standard English common noun.

Diacritical marks—accent marks, if you prefer—are the little doodads with which many foreign-derived words are festooned, generally above letters (mostly vowels), in some cases below them (that ç in "façade," for instance), and in other cases, especially in certain Eastern European languages, through them. In written English they're occasionally omitted, and the dictionary will often give you permission to skip them, but sojourning in a chateau can't be nearly as much fun as sojourning in a château, and if you send me your resume rather than your résumé, I'm probably not going to hire you.

But here's an idea: Let's say you're writing a novel in which the characters shimmy easily between English and, say, Spanish. Consider not setting the Spanish (or what have you) in italics. Use of italics emphasizes foreignness. If you mean to suggest easy fluency, use of roman normalizes your text.

On the other hand, if you're writing a novel about, say, an isolated young Englishwoman living in Paris who is confounded by the customs, the people, and the language, it would certainly make good sense to set all the bits of French she encounters, in narration or dialogue, in italics. You want that French to feel, every time, strange.

No matter how you're styling your foreign-language

bits and pieces, foreign-language proper nouns are always set in roman, as, say:

Comédie-Française
Déclaration des Droits de l'Homme et du
    Citoyen
Galleria degli Uffizi
Schutzstaffel

If you find you must use a foreign tongue you're not familiar with, be aware that free online translation tools are about as dangerous as language gets. It may be true that it's a small world in cyberspace, but don't entrust your words to the ghost in the machine. What you have to say is too important.

CHAPTER 5

THE REALITIES OF FICTION

Good writing involves much more than attending to spelling, punctuation, and grammar, especially when it comes to fiction, where artistry, however you want to define that slippery concept, can outrank and outweigh notions of what might conventionally be deemed "correct." In fiction, a writer's voice—eccentric, particular, peculiar as it may be—is paramount.

That isn't to say that anything goes, or that you can get away with any flaw in your writing by claiming that "it's just my voice." Fiction may be fictional, but a work of fiction won't work if it isn't logical and consistent.

- Characters must age in accordance with the calendar—that is, someone asserted to have been born in May 1960 must then be twenty-five in May 1985, forty in May

2000, etc.—and at the same pace as other characters: Two characters who meet at the ages of thirty-five and eighteen cannot, in a later scene, be fifty and merely twenty-six. Grandparents and great-grandparents, I've occasionally noted, are often said to have lived decades out of whack, in either direction, with what is possible.

- Keep track of the passage of time, particularly in narratives whose plots play themselves out, crucially, in a matter of days or weeks. I've encountered many a Friday arriving two days after a Tuesday, and third graders in math class on what, once one adds up the various "the next day"s, turns out to be a Sunday.
- Your characters' height; weight; eye and hair color; nose, ear, and chin size; right- or left-handedness; etc., need to remain consistent.
- Stage management and choreography: Watch out for people going up to the attic only to shortly and directly step out onto the driveway; removing their shoes and socks twice over the course of five minutes; and drinking from glasses they quite

definitively set down, a few paragraphs earlier, in another room.[*]

• • •

Real-world details must also be honored. You may think that readers won't notice such things. I assure you they will.

- If you're going to set your story on, say, Sunday, September 24, 1865, make sure that September 24, 1865, was indeed a Sunday. There are any number of perpetual calendars online.[†] (Also remember that if you're rummaging through old newspaper archives to see what was going on on September 24, 1865, you'd do well to look at newspapers dated September 25, 1865—remember, there was no same-day news in 1865.)
- I recall copyediting a novel in which the protagonist made a journey by, respectively,

---

[*] As a rule, the consumption of beverages is not as interesting as many writers seem to think it is.

[†] I've bookmarked timeanddate.com.

cab, train, subway, and a second cab in
three hours that couldn't, as I proceeded
to plot it out with maps, timetables, and a
healthy respect for speed limits, possibly
have been completed in fewer than ten.

- If you're going to set your story in, say,
New York City, you'd better keep track
of which avenues guide vehicles south to
north and which north to south, and which
streets aim east and which west.

- You've likely noticed that the sun rises and
sets at different times over the course of a
year. Make sure you remember to notice
that when you're writing.

- Not all trees and flowers flourish
everywhere on earth.

- If you want to be precise about characters'
moviegoing and TV-watching habits,
as many writers seem intent on doing,
make sure that, say, *Harry Potter and the
Sorcerer's Stone* was in theaters in the
summer of 2001[*] or that *Friends* aired
on Wednesdays.[†] If you're not up for that

---

[*] It was. You can find your own way to IMDb.
[†] It didn't. It aired on Thursdays. Wikipedia is great for this sort of thing.

sort of thing, you always have the option
of giving less rather than more detailed
information, or you can just make up
plausible-sounding movies and TV series,
which is a lot more fun anyway.

- Dictionaries are particularly helpful in
providing the first known use of any given
word, so if historical accuracy is important
in your novel, use one. Did you know, for
instance, that in the mid-nineteenth century,
someone who drank too much alcohol one
night might, the next morning, wake up
to a katzenjammer? The term "hangover"
didn't pop up till around 1894.

The Basics of Good Storytelling

Many writers rely more heavily on pronouns than is
strictly useful. For me this sort of thing comes under
the heading Remember That Writing Is Not Speaking.
When we talk, we can usually make ourselves understood even amid a flood of vague "he"s and "she"s. On
the page, too many pronouns are apt to be confounding.
I'd strongly suggest, to the point of insistence, that you
avoid referring to two people by the same pronoun over
the course of a single sentence; to be frank, I'd suggest

that you avoid it over the course of a single paragraph. The repetition of characters' names is one possible fallback, and though you as a writer may initially think that that third "Zoe" over the course of seven sentences is overkill, readers will be happier not to have to puzzle over which "she" you're talking about. On the other hand, if your paragraph is awash with names and pronouns and you think it's all too much, hunker down and do the sort of revision that eliminates the need for an excess of either. It can be tricky, but it's worth it, and it may well net you a leaner, stronger bit of prose.

- If your attempts to distinguish between unnamed characters of no particular importance lead to describing what "the first girl" said or did to "the second girl," you might want to step back and give these young women, if not names, at least distinct physical characteristics that can be expressed in one or two words. The redhead. The girl with glasses. Something.

- One writer of my beloved acquaintance possesses, it seems, only one way to denote an indeterminate number of things: "a couple." And not even "a couple of." No, it's a couple hours, a couple days, a couple cookies, a couple guys. I urge you to strive for variation. A few! Several! Some!

- When you've come up with that distinctive, wow-that's-perfect adjective, you may be so pleased with it that you unwittingly summon it up again right away. If your character says an idea is gut-wrenching on page 27, she shouldn't call some other idea gut-wrenching on page 31.* At the same time, be careful if you decide to use a thesaurus. Sometimes a show-offy word can scream "I LOOKED THIS UP!" Is that same character likely to call an idea "abhorrent," "vile," or "odious"? Don't use words that don't work within the context of your writing.

- Keep an eye on the repetition of even garden-variety nouns, verbs, adjectives, and adverbs of only moderate distinction, which you might not want to repeat in proximity—unless you're doing this with a purpose, in which case: Do it.

---

* I was recently advised of a novel in which the word "spatulate"— I didn't recognize it either; it's an adjective that means "shaped like a spatula"—showed up twice in two pages, referring to two entirely unrelated nouns. Oh dear.

Here is a marvelous example. I've always cherished it, and I like to haul it out whenever I can.

When Dorothy stood in the doorway and looked around, she could see nothing but the great gray prairie on every side. Not a tree nor a house broke the broad sweep of flat country that reached the edge of the sky in all directions. The sun had baked the plowed land into a gray mass, with little cracks running through it. Even the grass was not green, for the sun had burned the tops of the long blades until they were the same gray color to be seen everywhere. Once the house had been painted, but the sun blistered the paint and the rains washed it away, and now the house was as dull and gray as everything else.

When Aunt Em came there to live she was a young, pretty wife. The sun and wind had changed her, too. They had taken the sparkle from her eyes and left them a sober gray; they had taken the red from her cheeks and lips, and they were gray also. She was thin and gaunt, and never smiled, now. When Dorothy, who was an orphan, first came to her, Aunt Em had been so startled by the child's laughter that she would scream and press her hand upon her heart whenever Dorothy's merry voice reached her ears; and she still looked at the little girl with wonder that she could find anything to laugh at.

Uncle Henry never laughed. He worked hard from morning till night and did not know what joy was. He was gray also, from his long beard to his rough boots, and he looked stern and solemn, and rarely spoke.

It was Toto that made Dorothy laugh, and saved her from growing as gray as her other surroundings. Toto was not gray; he was a little black dog, with long silky hair and small black eyes that twinkled merrily on either side of his funny, wee nose. Toto played all day long, and Dorothy played with him, and loved him dearly.

Gray, gray, gray. Nine of them over the course of four paragraphs. They don't make a lot of noise—would you have noticed them if I hadn't set you looking for them?—but they get the job done.[*]

- Even a "he walked up the stairs and hung up his coat" might, if you're so inclined, benefit from a tweak—easy in this case: Just change "walked up" to "climbed."[†] I'll extend this advice even to the suggestion that you avoid echoing similar-sounding words: a "twilight" five words away from a "light," for instance.[‡]

- Be wary of inadvertent rhymes, of the "Rob commuted to his job" or "make sure that tonight is all right" sort. By "be wary," I mean: Don't do them.

- With all the nodding and head shaking going on, I'm surprised that half the

[*] Hoorah for L. Frank Baum and *The Wonderful Wizard of Oz,* of which these paragraphs are (nearly) the opening.

[†] Beyond eliminating the "up" repetition, you've also replaced a prepositional phrase with a more precise single-word verb, which almost invariably declutters and improves a sentence.

[‡] How bothersome are these tiny repetitions to your average reader? I don't know, but as a copy editor I'm highly aware of them and will always point them out. Beyond that it's up to the writer.

characters in modern fiction haven't
dislocated something. By the way,
characters who nod needn't nod their
heads, as there's really not much else
available to nod. And the same goes for
the shrugging of unnecessarily mentioned
shoulders. What else are you going to
shrug? Your elbows?

- If everyone in your world is forever pushing
their glasses up their collective noses,
please send everyone and their glasses to an
optician's shop.

- How often do you stare into the middle
distance? Me neither.

- A brief, by no means exhaustive list of
other actions that wise writers should
avoid:

> the angry flaring of nostrils
> the thoughtful pursing of lips
> the quizzical cocking of the head
> the letting out of the breath you didn't
> even know you were holding
> the extended mirror stare, especially
> as a warm-up for a memory whose

> recollection is apt to go on for
> ten pages

Also overrated:

blinking
grimacing
huffing
pausing (especially for "a beat")
smiling weakly
snorting
swallowing
doing anything wistfully

- "After a moment," "in a moment,"
  "she paused a moment," "after a long
  moment" . . . There are so many moments.
  So many.
- For fiction written in the past tense, here's
  a technique for tackling flashbacks that I
  stumbled upon years ago, and writers I've
  shared it with tend to get highly excited: Start
  off your flashback with, let's say, two or three
  standard-issue "had"s ("Earlier that year,
  Chad had visited his friend in Boston"), then

clip one or two more "had"s to a discreet "'d" ("After an especially unpleasant dinner, he'd decided to return home right away"), then drop the past-perfecting altogether when no one's apt to be paying attention and slip into the simple past ("He unlocked his front door, as he later recalled it, shortly after three o'clock"). Works like a charm.

- You writers are all far too keen on "And then," which can usually be trimmed to "Then" or done away with entirely.
- You're also overfond of "suddenly."
- "He began to cry" = "He cried." Dispose of all "began to"s.
- My nightmare sentence is "And then suddenly he began to cry."

Dialogue and Its Discontents

- Fond as I am of semicolons, they're ungainly in dialogue. Avoid them.
- In real-life conversation, how often do you say the name of the person you're talking to?

  Not that much?

  Then why do your characters do it so frequently?

- There's an awful lot of murmuring in fiction nowadays. There's also, I note, a great deal of whispering, quite a lot of it hoarse. You might offer your hoarse whisperer a cup of tea or a lozenge.
- Italics for emphasis in dialogue can be helpful, but use them sparingly. For one thing, readers don't always relish being told, in such a patently obvious fashion, how to read. For another, if the intended emphasis in any given line of dialogue can't be detected without the use of italics, it's possible that your given line of dialogue could use a bit of revision anyway. Among other solutions, try tossing the bit that needs emphasis to the end of a sentence rather than leaving it muddling in the middle.
- Go light on exclamation points in dialogue. No, even lighter than that. Are you down to none yet? Good.*
- I'll wager your characters can make

---

* There's a different standard for graphic novels. You'd still do well to limit use of exclamation points, but they're an expected and accepted convention in that genre. You'll also see double punctuation in graphic novels, but you should never see it—or use it—outside of that. Pick one punctuation mark and use it confidently.

themselves heard without capital letters. Use italics for shouting, if you must. And, yes, exclamation points—one at a time. No boldface, please, not ever.

- One especially well-attended school of thought endorses setting off dialogue with nothing fancier than "he said" and "she said." I've encountered enough characters importuning tearily and barking peevishly (phenomena that often result from the injudicious use of the thesaurus I mentioned above) that I'm not unsympathetic to that suggestion of restraint, but there's no reason to be quite so spartan should your characters occasionally feel the need to bellow, whine, or wheedle. Please, though: moderation. A lot of this:

> he asked helplessly
> she cried ecstatically
> she added irrelevantly
> he remarked decisively
> objected Tom crossly
> broke out Tom violently

is hard to take.

- If your seething, exasperated characters must hiss something—and, really, must they?—make sure they're hissing something hissable.

> "Take your hand off me, you brute!"
> she hissed.
> —CHARLES GARVICE,
> *Better Than Life* (1891)

Um, no, she didn't. You try it.

> "Chestnuts, chestnuts," he hissed.
> "Teeth! teeth! my preciousss; but
> we has only six!"
> —J.R.R. TOLKIEN,
> *The Hobbit* (1937)

OK, now we're cooking.

- Inserting a "she said" into a speech after the character's been rattling on for six sentences is pointless. If you're not setting a speech tag before a speech, then at least set it early on, preferably at the first possible breathing point.

- Something, something, something, she thought to herself.

  Unless she's capable of thinking to someone else—and for all I know your character is a telepath—please dispose of that "to herself."

- In olden times, one often saw articulated thought—that is, dialogue that remains in a character's brain, unspoken—set in quotation marks, like dialogue. Then, for a while, italics (and no quotation marks) were all the rage. Now, mostly such thoughts are simply set in roman, as, say:

  I'll never be happy again, Rupert mused.

  As it's perfectly comprehensible, and as no one likes to read a lot of italics, I endorse this.

- Speaking of articulated thought, I'm not entirely persuaded that people, with any frequency, or at all, blurt out the thoughts they're thinking.

  And when they do, I doubt very

much that they suddenly clap their
hands over their mouths.
- "Hello," he smiled.
  "I don't care," he shrugged.

  No.
  Dialogue can be said, shouted,
  sputtered, barked, shrieked, or
  whispered—it can even be murmured—
  but it can't be smiled or shrugged.
  The easiest solutions to such things
  are:

  "Hello," he said with a smile.
  "Hello," he said, smiling.

  or the blunter

  "Hello." He smiled.

  The better solution is not to employ
  these constructions in the first place.

A Few Pointers on Unfinished Speech

- If one of your characters is speaking and is cut off in midsentence by the speech or action of another character, haul out a dash:

  > "I'm about to play Chopin's Prelude in—"
  > Grace slammed the piano lid onto Horace's fingers.

- When a line of dialogue is interrupted by an action, note that the dashes are placed not within the dialogue but on either side of the interrupting action.

  > "I can't possibly"—she set the jam pot down furiously—"eat such overtoasted toast."

- If one of your characters is speaking and drifts off dreamily in midsentence, indicate that not with a dash but with an ellipsis.

> "It's been such a spring for daffodils,"
> she crooned kittenishly.[*] "I can't
> recall the last time . . ." She drifted
> off dreamily in midsentence.

- When characters self-interrupt and immediately resume speaking with a pronounced change in thought, I suggest the em dash–space–capital letter combo pack, thus:

> "Our lesson for today is— No, we
> can't have class outside today, it's
> raining."[†]

- "Furthermore," he noted, "if your characters are in the habit of nattering on for numerous uninterrupted paragraphs of dialogue, do remember that each paragraph of dialogue

---

[*] I originally wrote "such a *summer* for daffodils." My copy editor corrected me.

[†] The speaker just comma-spliced, and I feel fine about that. The occasional comma splice isn't going to kill anyone. You could, if you chose, break up that last bit into two sentences, but it's not as effective, nor does it quite convey the intended sound of the utterance.

concludes without a closing quotation mark, until you get to the last one.

"Only then do you properly conclude the dialogue with a closing quotation mark.

"Like so."

Miscellaneously

- If you're writing a novel in English that's set, say, in France, all of whose characters are supposed to be speaking French, do not pepper their dialogue with actual French words and phrases—*maman* and *oui* and *n'est-ce pas*. It's silly, cheap, obvious, and any other adjectives you might like if they'll stop you from doing this sort of thing. (Whenever I encounter these bits of would-be local color, I assume that the characters are suddenly speaking in English.)
- Conversely, real-life nonnative speakers of English, I find, rarely lapse into their native tongue simply to say yes, no, or thank you.
- And I implore you: Do not attempt, here in the twenty-first century, to convey

the utterance of a character who may be speaking other than what, for the sake of convenience, I'll call standard English with the use of tortured phonetic spellings, the relentless replacement of terminal g's with apostrophes, or any of the other tricks that might have worked for Mark Twain, Zora Neale Hurston, or William Faulkner but are, I assure you, not going to work for you. At best you'll come off as classist and condescending; at worst, in some cases, you'll tip over into racism.

A lot can be accomplished in the conveyance of eccentricity of speech with word choice and word order. Make good use of those.

- I've mentioned this before, and it applies to all writing, but I think it applies especially to fiction: Reading your writing aloud highlights strengths and exposes weaknesses. I heartily recommend it.

PART II

THE STUFF IN THE BACK

CHAPTER 6

NOTES ON, AMID A LIST OF, FREQUENTLY AND/OR EASILY MISSPELLED WORDS

A lot of people don't type with autocorrect or spell-check turned on—or pay attention even if they do. That said, neither* autocorrect nor spellcheck can save you from typing a word that is indeed a word but doesn't happen to be the word you mean or should mean to type. For more on that, see Chapter 8: The Confusables.

It goes without saying, though I'm happy to say it, that no one expects you to memorize the spelling of

---

* Please note the first word in this chapter to give the lie to the "*i* before *e*, except after *c*" rule ("or when sounding like *a*, as in 'neighbor' or 'weigh,'" the rule continues). There are any number of perfectly common words in the English language featuring the *ei* combination with no *c* (or *a* sound) in sight, from "foreign" to "heist" to "seizure" to "weird." To say nothing of "albeit" and "deify."

every word in the notoriously irregular, unmemorizable English language. My desk dictionary of choice, as I've mentioned oh so many times by now, is the eleventh edition of *Merriam-Webster's Collegiate Dictionary* (affectionately known as *Web 11*). You can find a number of first-rate dictionaries online, including Merriam-Webster's own (merriam-webster.com) and the densely helpful Free Dictionary (thefreedictionary.com).

Still, I do think that knowing how to spell on your own is a commendable skill, so I offer you a selection of the words I most frequently encounter misspelled— some of which I've been known to mess up myself— with remarks on some of the general issues of the art of spelling and its pitfalls.

ACCESSIBLE *(EASILY REACHABLE OR UNDERSTANDABLE)*
The "-ible" words and the "-able" words are easily confusable, and I'm afraid there's no surefire trick for remembering which are which. Though it is the case that most of the "-able"s are words in their own right even if you delete the "-able" (e.g., "passable," "manageable") and that most of the "-ible"s are not, shorn of their "-ible," freestanding (e.g., "tangible," "audible"), most is not all. As, to be sure, our friend "accessible." And see "confusable," seven lines up. "Confus"?

ACCOMMODATE *(TO MAKE ROOM FOR)*, **ACCOMMODATION**
(HOUSING, OR AN ADAPTATION MADE FOR CONVENIENCE OR
CONSIDERATION)

Words with double *c*'s are troublemakers; words with double *c*'s and double *m*'s are invitations to catastrophe.

ACKNOWLEDGMENT *(RECOGNITION)*

This is the preferred American spelling. The Brits favor (but not by much and only relatively recently) "acknowledgement."[*]

AD NAUSEAM

Latin for "to sickness," meaning "to excess": She bragged about her trip to Europe ad nauseam." Not spelled "ad nauseum."

AFICIONADOS *(LOVERS OF: THEY ARE AFICIONADOS OF*
MANGA; THEY COLLECT AS MANY BOOKS AS THEY CAN.)

One *f*, please. And note no *e* after the *o* in the plural form.

---

[*] Evidence also indicates that our British cousins are not as fond of the spelling "judgement" as some of them believe or would have you believe. And here is where I send you off (you'll find out why when you get there) to explore the Google Books Ngram Viewer, though I warn you that it's a direly addictive toy.

Spelling FAQ

Q. How do I know which words ending in *o* are pluralized with an *s* and which are pluralized with an *es*?

A. You don't. Look 'em up.

ASSASSIN *(KILLER)*, ASSASSINATE *(TO KILL)*, ASSASSINATED (KILLED), ASSASSINATION (KILLING)
Don't stint on the *s*'s.

BATTALION *(MILITARY DIVISION)*
Two *t*'s, one *l,* not the other way around. Think "battle," if that helps you.

BOOKKEEPER *(ONE WHO KEEPS TRACK OF FINANCES)*
The only legitimate English word I'm aware of that includes three consecutive sets of double letters,[*] and in writing it you're quite apt to forget the second *k*.[†]

---

[*] Well, yes, "bookkeeping." No, "sweet-toothed" doesn't count.
[†] Or, if you prefer, the first *k*.

BUOY *(FLOATING OBJECT ATTACHED TO THE BOTTOM OF A BODY OF WATER)*, BUOYANCY *(ABILITY TO FLOAT)*, BUOYANT *(ABLE TO FLOAT)*

That odd *uo*, which somehow never looks right, is easy to flip; thus my periodic encounters with "bouy," "bouyancy," and "bouyant."

BUREAUCRACY *(SYSTEM OF KEEPING ORDER, OFTEN A COMPLICATED AND ANNOYING ONE)*

First you have to nail down the spelling of "bureau," which is hard enough. Once you've conquered "bureau," you can likely manage "bureaucrat" and "bureaucratic," but be careful not to crash and burn, as I often do, on "bureaucracy," which always wants to come out "bureaucrasy."

CAPPUCCINO *(ESPRESSO WITH FROTHED MILK)*

Two *p*'s and two *c*'s.

Also, there is no *x* in "espresso," but you knew that already.

CENTENNIAL *(100TH)*

And its cousins "sesquicentennial" (150th)[*] and "bi-centennial" (200th).

CHAISE LONGUE

That's indeed how you spell it, because that's what it is—literally, from the French, a long chair. But the spelling "chaise lounge" took root in English, especially American English, an awfully long time ago, and it's not going anywhere, and one would be hard-pressed anymore to call it an error, particularly when it turns up in novels in the dialogue of characters who would not naturally say "chaise longue."

COMMANDOS (MILITARY PERSONNEL TRAINED FOR SPECIAL RAIDS)

My—and most people's—preferred plural of "commando." (Though "commandoes," which suggests to me a troop of female deer packing Uzis, is, per the dictionary, less incorrect than "aficionadoes.")

---

[*] I'm not sure why English needs a dedicated word for a 150th anniversary, but if it has a word for the thing before the thing before the final thing[†] and a word for jumping or being shoved out a window,[‡] why not.

[†] "Antepenultimate."

[‡] "Defenestration."

CONSENSUS (AGREEMENT)

Not "concensus."

DACHSHUND (WIENER DOG)

Two *h*'s.

DE RIGUEUR

From the French. A fancy-schmancy adjective meaning "required or prescribed by fashion."

DIETICIAN, DIETITIAN (NUTRITION SPECIALIST)

They're both correct. The latter is vastly more popular, though somehow I think the former better evokes the hairnets and lab coats of the elementary school lunch ladies of my distant youth.

DILEMMA (PUZZLE)

Ask a roomful of people whether at any time in their lives they believed this word to be spelled "dilemna," and you will receive in return quite a number of boisterous yeses. But the word is not spelled that way; it's never been spelled that way. So why does it so often end up as "dilemna"? It remains a mystery.

DIPHTHERIA (SERIOUS BACTERIAL INFECTION
AFFECTING THE NOSE AND THROAT)
Not "diptheria." There are two *h*'s here.

DOPPELGÄNGER
German for "double goer," meaning "twin," and not necessarily an evil twin, though the word somehow has a sinister ring. The popular error is to transpose the *el* to an *le*.

DUMBBELL (HAND WEIGHT)
Double *b*. The odds are good that left to your own devices you're going to spell this "dumbell," as you're also likely to attempt "filmaker," "newstand," and "roomate." Well, don't.

ECSTASY (BLISS)
Not "ecstacy." Perhaps you're confusing it with bureaucracy.

ENMITY (ILL WILL)
I was well into my twenties before I realized that this word was neither pronounced nor spelled "emnity." I have since learned—and I find it retroactively comforting—that I was not, and am not, the only victim of that misapprehension.

FASCIST (ONE IN FAVOR OF STRONG CENTRAL CONTROL
OF GOVERNMENT)
Capitalized when referring to an actual member of
Benito Mussolini's Fascisti in Italy during the 1930s, the
British Union of Fascists, or any other organization that
thus self-identifies, otherwise lowercased.*

FILMMAKER, FILMMAKING
Noted above, under "dumbbell," yet given the frequency
with which I encounter "filmaker" and "filmaking," apparently worth repeating.

FLUORESCENCE (BRIGHTNESS), FLUORESCENT
There's that peculiar *uo* again.

FLUORIDE (CHEMICAL COMPOUND THAT HELPS KEEP
TEETH HEALTHY)
And once again.

FORTY (THE NUMBER AFTER THIRTY-NINE)
Rarely to never misspelled on its own, but there's something about a follow-up "four" that leads, occasionally,

---

* A, perhaps randomly, I always refer to capital-N Nazis, even those who
are not of Hitler's political party. B, using the word in supposed jest, as
in calling your teacher a "homework Nazi," is both direly insulting and
offensively trivializing.

to "fourty-four." Use logic: it's not threety-three or fivety-five.

FUCHSIA (INTENSE PURPLE-RED)

Commonly misspelled "fuschia," a dishonor to the botanist Leonhard Fuchs, after whom the flower (and color) are named.

GENEALOGY (ANCESTRY)

I once let this go to print as "geneology" (perhaps I was thinking of geology?), and decades later the memory still stings.

GLAMOUR (ALLURE), GLAMOROUS

When Noah Webster was standardizing American English in the nineteenth century and streamlining "neighbour" into "neighbor," "honour" into "honor," etc., he neglected to transform "glamour" into "glamor"—because, oddly enough, he didn't include the word at all, in any form, in his initial 1828 dictionary or in any of his follow-up volumes. "Glamor" does show up from time to time, but certainly it lacks glamour. Do note, though, that "glamorous" is spelled only thus; it's never "glamourous." And it's "glamorize," never "glamourize."

GRAFFITI (UNAPPROVED ART OR WRITING ON A PUBLIC SURFACE)

Two *f*'s rather than, as I occasionally run across it, two *t*'s. It's a plural, by the way. There is a singular, "graffito," but no one ever seems to use it. Perhaps because one rarely encounters a single graffito?

GUTTURAL (LOW AND RASPY)

Not "gutteral," even though that's how you pronounce it. If you've studied any Latin, you may recognize this word that refers to throaty or generally disagreeable utterances as deriving from *guttur,* the Latin for "throat." If you haven't studied any Latin, you'll simply have to remember how to spell it.

HEROES

When one is writing about valiant champions, the plural of "hero" is, invariably, "heroes." The plural of the hero that's the heavily laden sandwich can be given, per the dictionary, as "heros," but I can't say I've run across it much if at all in the wild, and I can't say I care for it.

HIGHFALUTIN

This adjective, used to describe the putting on of airs, seems (even the dictionary isn't positive) to derive from a merger of "high" and "fluting"; nonetheless there's no apostrophe at its tail end (or, for that matter, a hyphen in its middle).

HORS D'OEUVRE, HORS D'OEUVRES (APPETIZERS)
Another French word. This one is a nightmare for everyone because of the *oeu*. Drill *oeu* into your head and the rest falls into place. The *s* for the plural is an English-language innovation; French makes do with *hors d'oeuvre* as both singular and plural.

While we're here: Though hors d'oeuvres include all more or less bite-size thingamabobs passable on trays, canapés are a subset of hors d'oeuvres requiring a base of bread, toast, cracker, puff pastry, etc., topped or spread with a topping or a spread. Amuse-bouches, which can be made out of just about anything so long as it's little, are chef-bestowed pre-meal[*] gifts, often served in those charming miniature ladle-like spoons. Now you know.

Using "appetizer" is generally safe.

---

[*] Modern style favors ditching the hyphen in words formed with prefixes (e.g., "antiwar," "postgraduate," "preoccupation," "reelect"), but if the result is difficult to read and/or uncommon, you should feel free to hold on to that hyphen. (The same goes for suffixes, as in the word "hyphenlessly," used back in Chapter 2.) Thus I opt for "pre-meal" rather than "premeal." (I find the universally accepted "premed" hard enough to make out on the first go, much less "premeal.") You'll note as well, when you cast your eye back up to the text proper, that I chose "ladle-like," as (though the likes of, say, "catlike" or "cakelike" is dandy) "ladlelike" would, I think, try your eyes' patience. (P.S. You can't ever do "dolllike," because look at it.)

HYPOCRISY (SAYING OR BELIEVING ONE THING BUT
DOING ANOTHER)
It's not "hypocricy." (See also "bureaucracy," above.)

IDIOSYNCRASY (PECULIARITY)
More of the same.

INDUBITABLY (UNDOUBTEDLY)
There's a *b* in the middle, not a *p*.

INFINITESIMAL (TINY)
Just the one *s*.

INOCULATE (VACCINATE AGAINST)
One *n* and one *c* only.

ITS, IT'S
You'll see this again later, but it bears repeating. "Its" is
a possessive adjective. "It's" is a contraction for "it is."
Please, please get it right.

LEPRECHAUN (IRISH ELF)
It doesn't look much more sensible properly spelled than
misspelled, but there you have it.

LIAISON (CONNECTION)

A word with three consecutive vowels is just begging for trouble.

The relatively recent back-formation[*] "liaise" irritates a lot of people. I think it's dandy and useful.

MARSHMALLOW

Two *a*'s, no *e*'s.

MEDIEVAL (FROM THE MIDDLE AGES)

Even the Brits don't use "mediaeval" much anymore, much less mediæval.[†]

MEMENTO (SOUVENIR)

Not "momento." Think of memory, because you buy and/or hold on to a memento so as to remember something.

---

[*] A back-formation is a neologism—that is, a newly coined word—derived from an already existing word, generally by yanking off a bit at the beginning or the end. Among the many common back-formations in the English language: "aviate" (from "aviator"), "burgle" (from "burglar"), "laze" (from "lazy"), "tweeze" (from "tweezers") . . . Well, there are a lot of them. For all the back-formations that slip effortlessly into popular use, though, many are controversial: "conversate" and "mentee," for instance, both of which I find grotesque, and "enthuse," which I find harmless but which some people have loved to hate since it was coined nearly two hundred years ago.

[†] That fused-letter thing is called a ligature.

MILLENNIUM (1,000 YEARS), MILLENNIA (PLURAL
OF MILLENNIUM), MILLENNIAL (THESE DAYS MOST
COMMONLY USED TO REFER TO A PERSON BORN IN THE
1980S OR 1990S)

Two *l*'s, two *n*'s. In each. (Well, "millennial" has three
l's, but who's counting?) It's always fun online to catch
someone attempting to insult millennials yet unable to
spell "millennials."

MINUSCULE (TINY)

Not "miniscule," however much that seems to make
sense.

MISCHIEVOUS (PLAYFUL)

The spelling—and pronunciation—"mis-chee-vi-ous"
go back centuries, but they're persistently considered
nonstandard (i.e., wrong). They're also unbearably
cutesy. Woodland elves might opt for "mischievious";
the rest of us should not. The word is prounounced
"mis-chi-vous."

MISSPELL, MISSPELLED, MISSPELLING

To misspell "misspell" is, to borrow a phrase from the playwright Tennessee Williams,* slapstick tragedy.

MNEMONIC (MEMORY DEVICE)

It has nothing to do with pneumonia. And as with *phenomenon,* I cannot read or say this word without thinking of the Muppets' "Mahna Mahna" song.

NAÏVE (INNOCENT), NAÏVETÉ (INNOCENCE)

Though the dictionary might (begrudgingly) let you get away with dropping the accent marks, there's no fun in spelling "naïve" or "naïveté" without them, and "naivety," though ratified by the dictionary, is just plain sad-looking.

NEWSSTAND

Two *s*'s, please. Two.

---

* There's nothing to be gained by referring to the playwright Tennessee Williams as "the famous playwright Tennessee Williams." If a person is famous enough to be referred to as famous, there's no need to refer to that person as famous. Neither is there much to be gained by referring to "the late Tennessee Williams," much less "the late, great Tennessee Williams," which is some major cheese. I'm occasionally asked how long a dead person is appropriately late rather than just plain dead. I don't know, and apparently neither does anyone else.

NON SEQUITUR

Latin for "it does not follow"; used to point out a logical flaw. If someone asks you "What's your favorite color?" and you reply "My name is Olivia," you're guilty of a non sequitur—your answer does not follow the question. In any event, it's not spelled "non sequiter." Also: blue.

OCCURRED, OCCURRENCE, OCCURRING

Pretty much everyone can spell "occur." Pretty much no one can spell "occurred," "occurrence," or "occurring."

ODORIFEROUS, ODOROUS (SMELLY)

They're both words. So is "odiferous," for that matter, but one rarely runs across it. They all mean the same thing: stinking.*

OPHTHALMIC (RELATED TO THE EYE),

OPHTHALMOLOGIST (EYE DOCTOR), OPHTHALMOLOGY

(MEDICAL SCIENCE OF THE EYE)

Eye-crossingly easy to misspell.

OVERRATE (THINK TOO HIGHLY OF)

Also overreach, override, overrule, etc.

---

* Though "moist" often tops lists of the most viscerally unpleasant words in the English language, I turn my nose up at "stinky" and "smelly."

PARALLEL (EQUIDISTANT AND NEVER MEETING; SIMILAR), PARALLELED, PARALLELISM

As a young person, I desperately wanted "parallel" to be spelled "paralell" or at least "parallell"; somehow it never was.

PARAPHERNALIA (STUFF; ODDS AND ENDS)

That *r* just past the midpoint has a tendency to fall out. No one seems to pronounce it. And yet.*

PASTIME (HOBBY)

Just the one *t*. (If it helps, consider that the two words being combined are "pass" and "time," not "past" and "time.")

PEJORATIVE (DEROGATORY, NEGATIVE)

Perhaps confusing the contemptuous "pejorative" with the lying "perjury," some people attempt "perjorative."

---

* There's an interesting linguistic phenomenon called the silent medial *t* that occurs in words like *often, hasten,* and *soften* in which the *t* goes unpronounced. I suppose the *r* in *paraphernalia* could be called a silent medial *r*. "Silent medial *t*" sounds to me like the name of a secret society ("He wore the signet ring identifying him as a member of the silent medial *t*'s") or a muscular condition ("Of course you can't complete a pull-up; you have silent medial *t*'s").

PENDANT (SOMETHING THAT HANGS)

It's not that "pendent," as occasionally turns up when "pendant" is meant, isn't a word; it's that it's usually not the word you want. "Pendant" is a noun; "pendent" is an adjective meaning hanging or dangling—that is, what a pendant does. Pendulously.

PERSEVERE (PERSIST), PERSEVERANCE, PERSEVERANT

I note a tendency to slip an extra *r* in, just before the *v*.

PHARAOH (ANCIENT EGYPTIAN MONARCH)

Reading, a few years back, a facsimile first edition of Agatha Christie's 1937 novel *Death on the Nile*, I was amused to note an instance of the misspelling "pharoah," which till then I'd figured was a recent problem.* Apparently not.

PIMIENTO (VARIETY OF PEPPER)

The popular spelling "pimento" cannot be called incorrect, though copy editors will persist in changing it. Interestingly, Web 11 has a separate entry for "pimento cheese." It contains pimientos.

---

* I sometimes get emails from readers who've stumbled upon a typo in one of our books. I don't like typos any more than you do—I probably like them quite a bit less—but as long as there have been books, there have been typos. Nobody's perfect.

POINSETTIA (THE RED- OR WHITE-PETALED PLANT YOU
SEE EVERYWHERE AT CHRISTMAS)
Neither "poinsetta" nor "poinsietta."

PREROGATIVE (CHOICE)
It is not spelled "perogative," though it's often misspelled—
and mispronounced—thus.

PROTUBERANCE (THING THAT STICKS OUT),
PROTUBERANT (STICKING OUT)
Not "protruberance" or "protruberant." Yes, you're
thinking of "protrude." We all are. That's why the misspelling keeps showing up.

PUBLICLY (IN PUBLIC!)
The vastly less popular "publically" is generally if not
universally held to be nonstandard, which is a nice way
of saying that by any decent standards it's incorrect.

RACCOON
The variant "racoon"—rarely seen now but once quite
popular—cannot be taken as incorrect, but it can surely
be taken as weird-looking.

RASPBERRY
With a *p*.

RENOWN (FAME), RENOWNED (FAMOUS)

Not "reknown" or "reknowned." The latter has always seemed especially cruel to me given that it means "well-known."

REPERTOIRE (SUPPLY), REPERTORY (THEATER COMPANY)

Three *r*'s each.

RESTAURATEUR (OWNER/OPERATOR OF A RESTAURANT)

It's not "restauranteur," and the floor is not open to debate as far as I'm concerned. I don't care what Webster's online says.

ROOMMATE

See "dumbbell" and "filmmaker," above. And just keep seeing them till you get these right.

SACRILEGIOUS (IRREVERENT OR DISRESPECTFUL)

You want to spell it "sacreligious." You can't.

SEIZE (TAKE OVER), SEIZED, SEIZURE

Easily and not infrequently misspelled, by people who get hung up on that "*i* before *e*" thing, as "sieze," "siezed," and "siezure." Maybe they're confusing it with "siege."

SEPARATE, SEPARATION

Not "seperate" and "seperation."

SHEPHERD

Some people may be named Shepard, but sheep watchers are shepherds and certain dogs are German shepherds and potato-crusted meat dishes are shepherd's pies.

SIEGE (ATTACK)

Even if you dodge the bullet of a misspelled "seize," you may still (counterintuitively) trip and misspell "siege" as "seige." Don't.

STOMACHACHE

It's peculiar-looking as one word, I suppose, but it sits cheek by jowl with "earache" and "headache," and no one seems to find them peculiar-looking at all.

STRAITJACKET

"Strait" as in constricted, not "straight" as in not curvy.[*] Also: straitlaced.

---

[*] The title of the 1964 Joan Crawford axe-murderess thriller—which you really ought to see—is *Strait-Jacket*. (The generally preferred American spelling is "ax," but I'd much rather be an axe-murderess than an ax-murderess. You?)

SUPERSEDE (TO TAKE THE PLACE OF SOMETHING)

Not "supercede." I have never in my life spelled "super-sede" correctly on the first try.

SURPRISE, SURPRISED, SURPRISING

In any of them, don't forget the first *r*, which is omitted with surprising frequency.

TAILLIGHT

Two *l*'s.

TENDINITIS (PAINFUL INFLAMMATION OF A TENDON)

Not "tendonitis," though that's likely an unstoppable re-spelling of the word (and I note that the local spellcheck has refused to call it out with the Red Dots of Shame).

THEIR, THERE, THEY'RE

"Their" is the possessive adjective. "There" is an adverb. "They're" is the contraction of "they are."

THRESHOLD (THAT WHICH YOU FIND UNDER A DOOR;
ALSO, GENERALLY, BOUNDARY)

It's not "threshhold." I bet you're thinking of "withhold."

UNDERRATE (TO PLACE TOO LOW A VALUE ON),
UNDERRATED, UNDERRATING
(And any other "under" + *r*–commencing compounds you can think of.)

UNWIELDY (HARD TO HANDLE)
Not "unwieldly," as I occasionally run across it. See *weird* below, which may be responsible.

VILLAIN, VILLAINOUS, VILLAINY
That's *ai,* not *ia.*

VINAIGRETTE (A CLASSIC DRESSING FOR SALADS)
Not "viniagrette." Also not, for that matter, "vinegarette."

WEIRD
I run across "wierd" more often than I ever expect to.

WHOA
It's been rendered online as "woah" so often that you might be persuaded that that's an acceptable alternate spelling. It is not.

WITHHOLD (KEEP AWAY)
See "threshold."

Y'ALL

It's *you* + *all,* so never "ya'll."

Somewhat to my Yankee surprise, there's scant consensus (and much feuding) among my Southern confederates as to whether "y'all" may properly be applied to just one person (and I leave discussion of the death-defying "all y'all" for another day) but near unanimity that non-Southerners shouldn't use it at all, y'all.

YOUR, YOU'RE

Like "its/it's": one is a possessive adjective, and one is a contraction. You're smart enough by now to know which is which.

WOULDN'T HAVE

It hurts to even say this, but not "wouldn't of." I beg you.

CHAPTER 7

PET PEEVES

I've never met a writer or other word person who didn't have a pocketful of language peeves—words or uses of words that drive a normally reasonable person into unreasonable outbursts of anger and irritation, if not fits of rage—and I doubt I'd trust anyone anyway who denied having a few of these bugaboos stashed away somewhere.

Everyone's pet peeves are different. The important thing to remember is that your own pet peeves reflect sensible preferences based on a refined appreciation of the music and meaning of the English language, and that everyone else's are the products of diseased minds.

OK, let's roll.

AGGRAVATE

If you use "aggravate" to mean not "make a bad thing worse" but "annoy intensely," though it has for centuries been used thus, you will irritate a goodly number of people, so you might well stick, in such cases, with "irritate." If "irritate" bores or otherwise aggravates you, use of one of its synonyms—among them "annoy," "exasperate," and, my favorite, "vex"—and save yourself the aggravation.

ANXIOUS

The utterly common and exceptionally long-established use of "anxious" to describe anticipation of a happy sort makes some people anxious, and not in a good way. As an anxious type myself, I don't think it's worth the kerfuffle. I reserve "anxious" for things I'm nervously battening down the hatches over and use "eager" to express, well, eagerness. That said, "anxious" comes in handy for things you're excited about that are nonetheless spawning stomach butterflies. A first date, say.

ARTISANAL

As can happen with any word that is suddenly, explosively ubiquitous, "artisanal," when used to refer to things made by hand for which you pay an arm and a leg, has quickly devolved from a selling point to an object of eye-rolling derision. Not being in the pickle, beer, or soap business, I rarely encounter it professionally, but if you're on the verge of using it, you might want to think twice. Then thrice.*

ASK

The nouning of the verb "ask"—"That's a big ask," "What's the ask on this?"—makes me chortle appreciatively, though I can't help but note that "request" is a perfectly charming word as either noun or verb. Verb-to-noun transformations—"nominalization" is the formal term for the process—can grate as well as amuse, as can many of the other attempts, often hailing from the worlds of business and academia, to gussy up shopworn ideas by replacing conventional language with overreaching—and arguably unnecessary—coinages.†

---

* This would have been the perfect place for a snickering reference to Brooklyn hipsters, but snickering references to Brooklyn hipsters are trite and tired, so I refrain. By the way, the rhetorical trick of referring to something by denying that you're referring to it is called apophasis. As in "Did you see her shirt? I won't even *mention* the skintight purple snakeskin pants." It's not as subtle as people pretend it is.

† Speaking out of the other side of my face, I might also argue that if you're not making up words every now and then, you're not doing your job. A brilliant man named Bertrand Russell, an intellectual jack-of-all-trades, wrote, "Language serves not only to express thoughts, but to make possible thoughts which could not exist without it." "Nouning," by the bye, is not one of mine. It's out there already.

BASED OFF OF

No. Just no. The inarguably correct phrase is "based on."

BEGS THE QUESTION

When used to mean "raises the question," this is not just a pet peeve; it's a nuclear threat. So duck and cover and listen up.

Begging the question, as the term is traditionally understood, is a logical fallacy in which someone argues for the legitimacy of a conclusion by citing as evidence the very thing they're trying to prove in the first place. Circular reasoning, that is. To assert, say, that vegetables are good for you because eating them makes you healthy or that I am a first-rate copy editor because clearly my copyediting improves other people's prose is to beg the question.

Except hardly anyone recognizes, much less uses, "begs the question" for that sort of thing anymore. The phrase has been overwhelmingly repurposed to mean "leads to an inevitable query," as in, "The undeniable failure of five successive big-budget special-effects-laden films begs the question, Is the era of the blockbuster over?"*

People who are in the business of hating the relatively new-fashioned use of "begs the question" hate it

---

* "Begs the question" has also taken on a part-time job to mean "evades the question," but I confront that vastly less frequently.

vehemently, and they hate it loudly. Unfortunately, subbing in "raises the question" or "inspires the query" or any number of other phrasings fools no one; one can always detect the deleted "begs the question."

BEMUSED

The increasing use of "bemused" to mean "wryly, winkingly amused" rather than "bothered and bewildered" is going to—sooner rather than later, I fear—render the word meaningless and useless, and that's too bad; it's a good word. My own never-say-die attitude toward preserving "bemusement" to mean perplexity, and only that, is beginning to give me that General Custer vibe.

CENTERED AROUND

Even as a spatially challenged person who doodled and dozed his way through geography class, I recognize that "centered around" doesn't make any sense, so I will always opt for "centered on" or "revolved around." You should too.

CHOMPING AT THE BIT

Yes, it's traditionally "champing at the bit." Yes, many people now write "chomping," likely because the word "champing" is unfamiliar to them. In that "champing" and "chomping" are as virtually indistinguishable in meaning as they are in spelling, the condemnation of "chomping" strikes me as trifling.

CLICHÉ

It's a perfectly lovely noun. As an adjective, it's annoying. You can afford the extra letter in "clichéd." Use it.

COMPRISE

I confess: I can barely remember which is the right way to use this word and which the wrong way, so every time I cross paths with it—or am tempted to use it—I stop to look it up.

"The English alphabet comprises twenty-six letters." This is correct.

"Twenty-six letters compose the English alphabet." This is also correct, though "make up" would sound a bit less stilted than "compose," don't you think?

"The English alphabet is comprised of twenty-six letters." Cue the sirens, because here come the grammar cops.

Use plain "comprise" to mean "made up of" and you're on safe ground. But as soon as you're about to attach the word "of" to the word "comprise," raise your hands to the sky and edit yourself. Once you've lowered your hands.

COULD CARE LESS

Use this phrase at your own peril to express utter indifference, because it inspires, from many, furious condemnation. (It's *couldn't* care less, people insist, because otherwise aren't you saying you do care? Logical but not inarguable.) I appreciate its indirect sarcasm, and the more people hate on it, the more apt I am to use it.

DATA

It's a plural, it's a singular, it's a breath mint, it's a dessert topping.

The data supports the consensus that "data" is popularly used as a singular noun, and it's worth neither fussing over this nor raising the existence of the word "datum."

Move on already.

DECIMATE

Because the Latin root of this word is *decem,* meaning "ten," some people would use "decimate" only to describe the punishment by death of one in ten—not one in nine, not one in eleven—mutinous soldiers.

Other people would use it to describe, generally, destruction.

The latter group certainly gets more use out of the word.

DIFFERENT THAN

There's nothing wrong with "different than," and don't let anyone tell you otherwise.

If you say "different to," you're likely a Brit, and that's OK too.

DISINTERESTED

I'd be happier if you'd restrict your use of "disinterested" to suggest impartiality and, when speaking of lack of interest, make use of the handy "uninterested." I don't think that's asking a lot.

EPICENTER

Strictly speaking, an epicenter is the place on the earth's surface directly above the place where an earthquake is occurring.

Less strictly speaking, an epicenter is a hub of activity, often but not always unhappy or unfortunate activity.

You're on relatively safe metaphorical ground referring to, say, the epicenter of a plague; a reference to Paris as the epicenter of classic cooking may not sit well on some stomachs.

I myself don't care much for fanciful uses of "epicenter," mostly because I think "center" does the job just fine.

FACTOID

If you use the word "factoid" to refer to a bite-size nugget of authentic information of the sort you'll find in a listicle,* you'll sadden those of us who hold to the word's original meaning: According to the writer Norman Mailer, who should certainly know because he was the one who invented the word in the first place, factoids are "facts which have no existence before appearing in a magazine or newspaper, creations which are not so much lies as a product to manipulate emotion in the Silent Majority." That the Great Wall of China is visible from the Moon is a factoid, as are the existence of George Washington's wooden teeth, the nationwide panic caused by Orson Welles's "War of the Worlds" broadcast, and the execution by burning at the stake of Salem's condemned witches.†

FEWER THAN/LESS THAN

The strict—and, really, not all that hard to remember—differentiation is that "fewer than" is applied to countable objects (fewer bottles of beer on the wall) and "less than"

---

* I love "listicle." If a coinage truly captures a concept for which no existing word will do, if it truly brings something fresh to the table, I say let it pull up a chair and make itself comfortable.

† Washington's dentures were made of ivory, metal, and teeth taken from animals and from other humans, including enslaved people; nah, it didn't; and (a) they weren't witches, and (b) they were hanged.

to what we call exclusively singular nouns (less happiness, less quality) and mass nouns (fewer chips, less guacamole).

Except—and there's always an "except," isn't there—you should use "less than" in discussions of distance (less than five hundred miles) and time (completing a test in less than sixty minutes—if you're not already saying "in under sixty minutes," which you probably are, and go ahead). And you likely use "less than" in discussions of money and weight: "I have less than two hundred dollars" or "I weigh less than two hundred pounds" or "a country that's gone to the dogs in less than five months," because it's not really the individual months you're interested in, but the swiftness of the decline.

To people who object to supermarket express-lane signs reading 10 ITEMS OR LESS: On the one hand, I hear you. On the other hand, get a hobby. Maybe flower arranging, or scrapbooking.

FIRSTLY, SECONDLY, THIRDLY

Like nails on a blackboard. Do you have blackboards anymore? OK, then . . . like feedback over a microphone.

If you decline to write "firstly," "secondly," and "thirdly" in favor of "first," "second," and "third," not only are you saving letters, but you can tell all your friends about this amazing thing called a flat adverb—an adverb that matches in form its sibling adjective, notably doesn't end in "-ly," and is 100 percent correct, which is why we're allowed to say "Sleep tight," "Drive safe," and "Take it easy." Though not in that order.

FOR ALL INTENSIVE PURPOSES

I didn't intend to include "for all intensive purposes" on this list because I've never, so far as I can recall, encountered anyone saying or writing it except as a joke about people saying or writing "for all intensive purposes." But it's out there (and has been since the 1950s), and it turns up intermittently in print.

It's "for all intents and purposes." It makes sense if you think about it: What would an "intensive purpose" be, anyway?

FORTUITOUS

As to the use of "fortuitous" to mean fortunate or favorable, it's universally acceptable so long as the good fortune or favor is accidental, because that's what "fortuitous" means: by chance (though, in its original sense, with no guarantee of a happy ending). If you achieve something good by the sweat of your brow, find a word that better honors your achievement.

FULSOME

A word that over the centuries has picked up more meanings than are good for it, or for you: among them abundant, generous, overgenerous, excessive, offensive, and stench-ridden. (It can also be applied to the sort of interior decorating taste that leans toward gilt and gold-plated everything, though the best word for that sort of thing remains the Yiddish word *ungapatchka*.) Though you may be tempted to apply "fulsome" unambiguously positively, if you allude to a "fulsome expression of praise," a hefty chunk of your audience will have visions of shameless brown-nosing dancing in their heads. So just skip it.

GIFT (AS A VERB)

If you're bored with "bestow," "proffer," "award," "hand out," "hand over," or any of the other excellent verbs the English language has come up with over the years to describe the act of giving a person a thing, by all means make use of "gift," which I wouldn't even consider describing as odious because I'm not that sort of person and because, I assure you, many other people are already lined up eagerly to do so.*

---

* "Regift," on the other hand, is a gorgeous coinage because it does something no other word can properly do.

GROW (TO MEAN "BUILD")

You can't argue, as some people attempt to do, that you can't properly use the phrase "grow a business" (rather, that is, than "build a business") because "grow" is only an intransitive verb (the sort that doesn't take an object). Why not? Because it is also, or at least can be, a transitive verb, as you'll surely note as you grow dahlias or a mustache.

You are free, though, to dislike such bureaucratese phrases as "grow the economy" because they are, to use the technical term, icky.

HOPEFULLY

If you can live with "There was a terrible car accident; thankfully, no one was hurt," you can certainly live with "Tomorrow's weather forecast is favorable; hopefully, we'll leave on time." Sticklers will insist that what you're really saying is "We will leave on time with hope" and that you should instead say "I'm hopeful that we'll leave on time."

"Thankfully" and "hopefully" are, in these uses, disjunct adverbs, meaning that they modify not any particular action in the sentence (as they would in, say, "she thankfully received the gift" or "he hopefully approached his boss for a raise") but the overall mood of the speaker of the sentence (or simply the sentence itself).

I'm not sure how "hopefully," among all such disjunct usages, got singled out for abuse, but it's unfair.

By the way, you may recognize the use of a disjunct adverb in one of the most famous lines ever delivered in a movie: "Frankly, my dear, I don't give a damn."

Ahem.

ICONIC

A word whose overuse has rendered it as dull and meaningless as "famous." Moreover, while "famous" is at least applied to people who are at least reasonably celebrated and widely recognized, "iconic" seems lately to be desperately applied to people who are barely even well known. It should be used to denote entities of singular importance.

IMPACT (AS A VERB)

The use of the verb "impact," in the sense of "affect," when "affect" might be perfectly appropriate and sufficient, is a true scream inducer. You may already be screaming.

I don't necessarily hold with the notion that the verb "impact" should never be used for anything less, um, impactful than an asteroid wiping out the dinosaur population, but do try to reserve it for big-ticket items.

IMPACTFUL

Yet another of those words that carry that unmistakable whiff of business-speak, and it's not, to my nose, a pleasant scent. If everyone stopped using it, I bet no one would miss it.

INVITE (AS A NOUN)

If your life expectancy is so limited that you don't have the time to issue an invitation, you might not be up to throwing that party.

IRONY

Funniness is not irony. Coincidence is not irony. Weirdness is not irony. Rain on your wedding day is not irony. Irony is irony: there's a disconnect between what's happening and what should be happening, or what's said and what's interpreted. If I tell you I went to the bank specifically to make sure my money was safe and was subsequently held up at gunpoint, that's irony.

IRREGARDLESS

This grim mash-up of "irrespective" and "regardless" is wholly unnecessary. Plus—and don't pretend otherwise—you know you use it only to irritate people.

LITERALLY

A respectable word that has been distorted into the Intensifier to End All Intensifiers. No, you did not literally die laughing. No, I don't care that all your cool friends use "literally" that way. Are all your friends literally rolling on the floor laughing? I doubt it.

MORE THAN/OVER

This distinction, specifically insofar as counting is concerned, is less controversial than that between "less than" and "fewer than," mostly because so few people observe it, and also because you'd be hard-pressed to find anyone in the word biz willing to defend it. So whether a book is over six hundred pages long or more than six hundred pages long, or whether little Jimmy is suddenly more than six feet tall or suddenly over six feet tall . . . Do as you like. It's nothing to get worked up more than.

NAUSEATED (VS. NAUSEOUS)

I don't think I knew till I was well beyond my college years that there was even such a word as "nauseated." On those occasions when I was about to heave, I was content to be nauseous. Eventually I learned the traditional differentiation between "nauseous"—causing nausea—and "nauseated"—preparing to heave—but it was too late for me to mend my ways, so I'm still happy, as it were, to be nauseous.

NONPLUSSED

So then, "nonplussed." To be nonplussed is to be confused, startled, at a loss for words. Lately the word's devolved into a synonym for relaxed, cool as a cucumber, chill, and that's a problem. How has this come to be? Presumably the "plussed" part strikes some eyes/ears as meaning "excited," so the "non" part seems to turn that on its head, and there you have "nonplussed" serving as its own antonym.

ON ACCIDENT

Yes, it's "on purpose." No, it's not "on accident." It's "by accident."

PASS AWAY

In conversation with a bereaved relative, you might, I suppose, refer to someone having passed away or passed. In straightforward writing, people die.

PENULTIMATE

"Penultimate" is not a fancy word for "ultimate." It does not mean "like totally ultimate, bro." It means "the thing before the last thing," or the next-to-last thing.

PERUSE

I've given up on "peruse," because a word that's used to mean both "read thoroughly and carefully" and "glance at cursorily" is as close to useless as a word can be.*

PLETHORA

People who use "plethora" to describe something of which there's too much—it started out in English as the name of a condition involving an overabundance of blood—sneer grimly at those who use it simply (and positively) to mean "a lot of something." Either way, it's fun to say.

REFERENCE (AS A VERB)

You can just say "refer to."

RESIDE

You mean "live"? For some reason, you'll see this word a lot if you read the About the Authors at the back of books or on the flaps. I think using "resides" rather than "lives" tells you a lot about the author.

---

* There are words called contranyms, or Januses, that also mean their opposite: dust (to sprinkle powder on OR to remove powder from), cleave (cling to OR separate from), trim (cut from OR add to). English is just cruel sometimes.

'ROUND

If she's approachin' by way of circumnavigatin' a mountain, she's comin' round it, and one can do nicely without an apostrophe before that *r*. I'm talking to you, people who like to write "'til" or, worse, "'till." (It's *till*, please.)

STEP FOOT IN

For your own safety, I'm telling you, just say "set foot in." You'll live longer.

'TIL

Once again, for the people in the cheap seats: "Till" is a word: till the cows come home. "Until" is a word: until the cows come home. "Till" is an older word than "until." They both mean the same thing. There's no justification whatsoever for "'til."

TRY AND

If you try *and* do something, someone will immediately tell you to try *to* do it, so you might as well just try *to* do it so no one will yell at you.

UTILIZE

You can haul out "utilize" when you're speaking of making particularly good use of something, as in utilizing facts and figures to project a company's future earnings, or using something in an unconventional fashion, as in utilizing a key to open a bottle of Coca-Cola. Otherwise all you really need is "use."

VERY UNIQUE

In the 1906 edition of *The King's English,* coauthors and brothers Henry Watson Fowler and Francis George Fowler declared—and they were neither the first nor the last people to so declare—"A thing is unique, or not unique; there are no degrees of uniqueness; nothing is ever somewhat or rather unique, though many things are almost or in some respects unique."

I will allow that something can be virtually unique but can't be more than—not very, not especially, not really—unique.

You might as well hang a KICK ME sign on your writing.*

---

* For other things that will render you kickable, see Chapter 11.

CHAPTER 8

THE CONFUSABLES

"When I use a word," Humpty Dumpty said,
in rather a scornful tone, "it means just what I choose
it to mean—neither more nor less."
"The question is," said Alice, *"whether you can make*
words mean so many different things."
"The question is," said Humpty Dumpty,
"which is to be master—that's all."
—LEWIS CARROLL, Through the Looking-Glass,
and What Alice Found There

Spellcheck is a marvelous invention, but as I've said, it can't stop you from using the wrong word when the wrong word you've used is a word (but the wrong word). Beware the following in particular.

A LOT/ALLOT, ALLOTTED, ALLOTTING

A lot of something is a great deal of it. (Please, please, not "alot." Ever. You'll see that in advertisements fairly often; those are the businesses you should boycott.)

To allot is to assign or mete out.

ADVANCE/ADVANCED

To advance is to move forward. The past tense of "advance" is "advanced."

An advance is a forward movement, as of an army, or a preliminary payment, as to writers who have not yet finished writing their books or children seeking to get ahead on their allowances.

As well, "advance" means beforehand (as in "supplied in advance").

On the other hand, "advanced" refers to being ahead of the norm in progress or complexity, as an exceptionally clever student (like you) is advanced.

ADVERSE/AVERSE

"Adverse" means unfavorable or harmful, as in "We are enduring adverse weather" or "I did well on my test under adverse circumstances."

"Averse" means opposed to, repulsed by, or antipathetic toward, as in "I am averse to olives on my pizza."

AFFECT/EFFECT

The traditional snap differentiation between "affect" and "effect" is that "affect" is a verb ("That rule is only for third graders, so it doesn't affect me at all") and "effect" is a noun ("That rule has no effect on me at all"). Which is true, but it's not the whole story.

Because "affect" is also a noun: "a set of observable manifestations of a subjectively experienced emotion." You may speak, for instance, of a psychiatrist's commenting on a traumatized patient's affect, or demeanor.

And "effect" is also a verb, as in "to effect change"—that is, to cause change to happen.

Other uses of these words and their variants—as an affected person affects a posh accent; your personal effects (the things you're carrying around on your person); "in effect" in the sense of "virtually"—seem to cause less confusion.

AID/AIDE

To aid is to help.

An aide is an assistant.

AISLE/ISLE

Aisles are the passages between seating areas in theaters and houses of worship and airplanes, and between shelves of groceries in supermarkets.

Isles are islands (usually small ones).

ALL RIGHT/ALRIGHT

Some people object to "alright" as slovenly, and its appearance in print remains rare relative to that of "all right." But the fact that I'm regularly asked my opinion of the acceptableness or un- of "alright" suggests to me that it's making inroads, like it or not. I continue to wrinkle my nose at the sight of it, perhaps because I can't see that it has a worthwhile-enough distinction from "all right" to justify its existence, as, say, "altogether" and "already" are distinctly distinct from "all together" and "all ready." You may feel otherwise.

ALLUDE/ALLUSION/ALLUSIVE/ELUDE/ELUSIVE

To allude is to hint at, as you might allude to a painful subject rather than discussing it explicitly.

An allusion is such an indirect, or allusive, reference.

To elude is to escape, as a bank robber eludes the police.

A dream you half-recall on waking that then slips entirely from your consciousness might be called elusive. That is, it's difficult to hold on to.

ALTAR/ALTER

An altar is a raised structure on which, in religious ceremonies, sacrifices are made or gifts are left.

To alter is to change.

ALTERNATE/ALTERNATIVE

The Strictly Speaking Club, of which I'm an on-again, off-again member, will tell you that, strictly speaking, an alternate is a thing that replaces a thing, and alternatives—

which travel in packs, or at least pairs—are options, any one of which might be viable. That is, if, owing to construction, I'm forced off the main stairs to school and must find my way inside via the side entrance, I'm mandated to travel an alternate route, but on another day, should I opt to make my way inside through the gym entrance instead of going in the front, I am simply choosing an alternative route.

As well, to do something every other Wednesday is to do that thing on alternate Wednesdays, to blow hot and cold in one's feelings is to alternately like and dislike something, and constructing a lasagna with tiers of noodles, sauce, and cheese is to build it with alternate layers. "Succeeding by turns," as the dictionary helpfully phrases it.

Also as well, an option beyond normalcy* is an alternative: alternative music, alternative medicine, alternative lifestyle, etc. (This use can carry a whiff of disapproval, so be careful how you apply it.)

One's alternate identity (Bruce Wayne's Batman, Beyoncé's Sasha Fierce, Stefani Joanne Angelina Germanotta's Lady Gaga) is one's alter ego.[†]

---

* Or normality, if you prefer that alternative.

† Pseudonyms are not alternate *identities* but simply alternate *names* used for professional, literary, political, or, occasionally, terroristic purposes: Currer Bell for Charlotte Brontë, Lewis Carroll for Charles Lutwidge Dodgson, Leon Trotsky for Lev Davidovich Bronstein, El Guapo for Alfonso Arau, etc.

AMBIGUOUS/AMBIVALENT

To be ambiguous is to lack clarity, to be murkily open to misinterpretation. Being ambiguous can also be diplomatic, as when you see a particularly unsightly dog and comment "Now, *that's* a dog."

To be ambivalent is to have mixed feelings.

Your meaning may be ambiguous, but your attitude is ambivalent.

AMOK/AMUCK

To run amok is, in its original sense, to launch, after a bout of brooding, into a murderous frenzy. "Amuck" is simply a variant spelling of "amok."

AMUSE/BEMUSE/BEMUSED

To amuse is to entertain, delight, divert.

To bemuse is to perplex, befuddle, preoccupy, nonplus.

The rising use of "bemused" to describe, as I noted earlier, a sort of wry, unflappable, tuxedo-wearing, cocktail-sipping amusement may be unstoppable, but unstopped it will certainly kill off the usefulness of the word entirely—just as the redefinition of "nonplus," which properly means to confuse-startle-unnerve, to mean its precise opposite ("I wasn't frightened at all; I was completely nonplussed"), will, unchecked, render that word unusable in any fashion. Don't say I didn't warn you.

ANYMORE/ANY MORE

"Anymore" = any longer or at this time, as in "I've a feeling we're not in Kansas anymore."

"Any more" = an additional amount, as in "I don't want any more pie, thank you."

You don't have to search back too many decades to find frequent use of "any more" where we would now, at least in America, write "anymore." (The Brits remain less keen on the fused version.)

APPRAISE/APPRISE

To appraise is to assess or evaluate, as one has a gem appraised to determine its worth.

To apprise is to inform, as you apprise your friends of your vacation plans.

ASSURE/ENSURE/INSURE

One person assures another person so as to relieve doubt: "I assure you we'll leave on time."

To ensure is to make something certain—some*thing,* not some*one:* "The proctor is here to ensure that there is no talking during the test."

"Insure" is best reserved for discussions of compensation in the event of death or theft, monthly premiums, and everything else involved in our betting that something terrible is going to happen to us.

BAITED/BATED

A trap or fishing line is baited—that is, outfitted with bait.

"Bated," which you are unlikely to chance upon disattached from the word "breath," means reduced or moderated or suspended. To await something with bated breath is to await it with thrilled tension, to be on (to use a grand old word) tenterhooks.

BAWL/BALL

To bawl your eyes out is to weep profusely.

To ball your eyes out would be some sort of sporting mishap.

BESIDE/BESIDES

"Beside" means "next to" (as in "Come sit beside me").

"Besides" means "other than" (as in "There's no one left besides Granny who remembers those old days").

I've found that "beside" is frequently used when "besides" is meant, and I wonder whether people who have had it drilled into their heads to use "toward" rather than "towards," "backward" rather than "backwards," etc., view "besides" as a Briticism-to-be-avoided. Or, thinking it a relative of "anyways," view it as an outright error.

BLACK OUT/BLACKOUT

The verb is "black out," as one may black out after a blow to the head.

The noun is "blackout," meaning a loss of consciousness, an electrical power failure, or a suppression of information (as in a news blackout).

BLOND/BLONDE

"Blond" is an adjective: He has blond hair; she has blond hair.

"Blond" and "blonde" are also nouns: A man with blond hair is a blond; a woman with blond hair is a blonde. "Blonde" carries some heavy cultural baggage by way of the old stereotype "dumb blonde," so use it thoughtfully and carefully, if at all.

BORN/BORNE

The word you want for discussions of birth, actual or metaphorical, is "born," whether you mean born yesterday, born in a trunk, or New York–born.

Otherwise, things that are carried or produced are borne. Diseases are insect-borne. A tree that bears fruit has borne fruit. The right to bear arms is the right to have borne them.

And though triumph may be born out of tragedy, your grand schemes may not be borne out in reality.

BREACH/BREECH/BROACH/BROOCH

To breach is to break open or pierce.

A breach is a rupture or violation, as in a breach in a dam or a breach of etiquette. When Shakespeare's Henry V cries, "Once more unto the breach, dear friends, once more," he's literally referring to the gap his English troops have opened in the walls of a French city under siege. Note, please, that it's "unto the breach," not, as it's often misquoted, "into" it.

A breach is also the leaping of a whale out of the ocean; the whale is said to be breaching.

"Breech" is an outmoded term for buttocks; thus pants were once called breeches. A breech birth is one in which the baby emerges buttocks (or feet) first.

To broach a subject is to raise it.

A brooch is a piece of decorative jewelry.

BREATH/BREATHE

"Breath" is a noun; "breathe" is a verb. One loses one's breath. One breathes one's last breath.

"Breath" is often written when "breathe" is called

for. This is an especially easy error to commit and, once committed, difficult to catch, so I urge you to be on your guard about it.

No one ever seems to get "breadth" wrong—though it comes up every now and then in "Hey, how come it's 'length' and 'breadth' and 'width' but not 'heighth'?" conversations*—so I simply note its existence.

CALLOUS/CALLUS
To be callous is to be hard-hearted.

A callus is a thickening of the skin.

Many, many, many people get this wrong, so if you can get it right you'll earn a slew of brownie points.†

CANVAS/CANVASS
Canvas is cloth, of the sort used to make sails or to paint on.

To canvass is to secure votes or opinions.

CAPITAL/CAPITOL
A capital is an important city, or a large letter as one would find at the beginning of a sentence or a proper

* It used to be "heighth" and now it's not, and these days "heighth" is generally characterized as "nonstandard" or "dialectical." How's that for an unsatisfactory answer?

† Whence the term "brownie points"? No one's 100 percent certain; it's one of those wonderful word mysteries. I like the idea that not everything can be or needs to be known.

noun, or one's accumulated funds, or, architecturally, the crown of the shaft of a column. It is also an adjective describing a serious crime (often, though not invariably, punishable by death) and something that approving British people used to exclaim—"Capital!"—before they all started exclaiming "Brilliant!"

A capitol is a building housing a legislature, like the great domed Capitol (capitalized in this case, as that is its name) in our nation's capital.

CARAT/KARAT/CARET/CARROT

A carat is a unit of weight applied to gemstones.

The proportion of gold in an alloy is measured in karats, the purest gold being 24-karat.

A caret is a copyediting and proofreading symbol (it looks like this: ^) showing where new text is to be inserted into an already set line.

Carrots are what Bugs Bunny eats.

CHORD/CORD

In music, a chord is a number of notes played simultaneously; "chord" is also used to refer to an emotional response, as a plaintive melody may be said to strike a chord.

A cord is a woven string of threads.

To strike a blow against an exceptionally popular

error: People have vocal cords, not (no matter how musical they are) "vocal chords."

CITE/SIGHT/SITE

The confusion between "cite" and "site" seems to be on the rise. To cite something is to quote or attribute it, as you cite a reference book or a website. And, aha, there's the potential for confusion: In citing a fact found on a (web)site, the desire to "site" it is increasingly compelling (but still incorrect).

Further confusion arises between "site"—as a noun, the property on which a structure is constructed; as a verb, the action of placing that structure—and "sight," a thing one goes to see, e.g., the sights of Paris one views while sightseeing.

A sight is also the dojigger on a firearm that helps you aim, thus "I've got you in my sights."

CLASSIC/CLASSICAL

A classic is an excellent or defining version of something, as "Hey Ya!" is a classic pop song by OutKast and the classic cure for hiccups is to hold your breath.

"Classical" is best reserved for descriptions of things like the civilizations of ancient Greece and Rome or the orchestral music of the eighteenth and nineteenth centuries. You know, things you write about every day.

CLIMACTIC/CLIMATIC

The former relates to narrative thrills, spills, and chills on the way to a story's resolution; the latter concerns, perhaps (and hopefully) less thrillingly, meteorological phenomena. The climactic moment of the September 2019 UN Climate Action Summit was Greta Thunberg's "How Dare You" speech asking world leaders to address climatic change.

COMPLEMENT/COMPLEMENTARY/COMPLIMENT/ COMPLIMENTARY

To complement something is to go nicely with it.

If I am telling you how great you look with your complementing backpack and shoes, I am paying you a compliment.

An ability to spell and an ability to type rapidly and accurately might be thought of as complementary skills in secretarial work—that is, each serves the other.

If I am offering you my spelling and typing skills free of charge, I am giving you access to a complimentary service.

CONFIDANT/CONFIDANTE

If you're not a fan of gendered nouns, you can certainly apply "confidant" to anyone with whom you share confidences. Just don't refer to a man as a confidante; confidantes are solely women.

(Most people discern correctly between "fiancé" and "fiancée," but most is not all.)

CONSCIENCE/CONSCIOUS

Your conscience is the little voice inside you that helps you differentiate between right and wrong. If you are Pinocchio in the Disney version, you possess an externalized conscience in the person—well, in the insect—of Jiminy Cricket.

To be conscious is to be awake and alert, also to be particularly aware and mindful.

CONTINUAL/CONTINUOUS

"Continual" means ongoing but with pause or interruption, starting and stopping, as, say, continual thunderstorms (with patches of sunlight) or continual bickering (with patches of truce).

"Continuous" means ceaseless, as in a Noah-and-the-Flood-like forty days and forty nights of unrelenting rain.

CRITERION/CRITERIA

"Criterion" is singular: a standard upon which one can make a decision. A number of criterions (it's a word, really, though I can't think of the last time I saw it used) are criteria.

I frequently encounter the plural "criteria" where the singular "criterion" is meant. Perhaps people think it's fancier. It's not meant to be fancy; it's meant to be a plural, and it should only be used as a plural. (It's a holdover from Latin, like "millennia" as the plural of "millennium" and "nuclei" as the plural of "nucleus.")

DEFUSE/DIFFUSE

To defuse is, literally, to remove a fuse, as from a bomb, to keep it from blowing up. Figuratively, if you're trying to calm down a roomful of arguing people, you're defusing a thorny situation.

The adjective "diffuse" means unconcentrated (as, say, "diffuse settlements in a vast territory"). As a verb it means "to spread" (as air freshener may diffuse, or be diffused, through a room). You buy an aromatherapy diffuser that spreads relaxing lavender or energizing grapefruit (or you ignore the "therapy" part and just buy something that makes your room smell better).

DEMUR/DEMURE/DEMURRAL

To demur is to voice opposition or objection; perhaps because the word, spoken, makes a gentle burring noise (or perhaps because it looks like "demure"), it's often used to suggest polite opposition, but politeness isn't inherent in the verb.

"Demur" is also a noun, as one may accept someone else's decision without demur.

To be demure is to be modest or reserved.

DESERT/DESSERT

Most of us can tell the difference between a desert (that hot and dry place) and a dessert (that sweet and soul-satisfying complement to a meal).

Many go wrong in their attempt to haul out the venerable* phrase referring to people who get what they deserve. Such people are getting not their "just desserts" but their just deserts—they are getting precisely what they *deserve*.

Though if you and your friends go to a diner with the sole intention of enjoying a couple of slices of pie and some milk shakes, you may be said to be receiving just desserts.

DISCREET/DISCRETE

Discreet people possess discretion; they kiss but don't tell. They are circumspect, chary, and wary. If you don't want people to know what you're doing, you do it discreetly.

---

* I've occasionally seen "venerable" used to mean, solely, eminent or to mean, solely, old. I'd say that it's best used to mean both, together.

This thing over here and that thing over there are discrete—separate and distinct—things. If you sample two distinct populations in your science experiment, you sample them discretely.

E.G./I.E.

Please don't confuse these. They're both Latin abbreviations; e.g. stands for *exempli gratia* and means "for example," while i.e. stands for *id est* and means "that is."

EEK/EKE

"Eek!" is what you exclaim when you see a mouse.

To eke (as in "to eke out a living") is to secure something with difficulty and, as a rule, barely. I suppose you could, if you were pretending to be frightened, eke out an eek.

EMIGRATE/IMMIGRATE

You emigrate from a place; you immigrate to a place. My paternal grandfather emigrated from Latvia; he immigrated to the United States. The terms are used to describe movement from one nation or continent to another; one does not, say, emigrate from Chicago to New York, or even from Chicago to Paris.

EMINENT/IMMINENT/IMMANENT

To be eminent is to be renowned, famous, usually respected.

To be imminent is to be on the way and arriving any moment now.

To be immanent is to be inherent—built in, so to speak. You'll usually see the term applied to constitutional rights and the existence and influence of God.

ENVELOP/ENVELOPE

"Envelop" is the verb, as in to surround or encompass, "envelope" the noun, as in the paper doohickey into which one puts a letter.

EPIGRAM/EPIGRAPH

An epigram is a succinct, smart, and, as a rule, humorous statement, of the sort Oscar Wilde used to toss about like Ritz crackers to ducks in the park. For instance, from the irresistibly quotable play *The Importance of Being Earnest:* "All women become like their mothers. That is their tragedy. No man does. That's his."

An epigraph is an evocative quotation—rarely humorous but generally succinct—set at the beginning of a book, often immediately after the dedication, or at the beginning of a chapter.

EVERYDAY/EVERY DAY

"Everyday" is an adjective ("an everyday occurrence"), "every day" an adverb ("I go to work every day").

"Everyday" is increasingly often being used as an adverb; this is highly bothersome, and please don't you dare speed up the trend.

EVOKE/INVOKE

To evoke is to call to mind, as the smell of coconut may evoke a fondly remembered tropical vacation or the songs of Bruno Mars may be said to evoke those of James Brown, the undisputed Godfather of Soul.

To invoke is to summon in actual practice, as a warlock invokes demons to destroy his enemy, or to call upon for protection or assistance, as you might invoke your Fifth Amendment right to remain silent and avoid self-incrimination.

To put it as simply as I can, if you confine evoking to the figurative and invoking to the actual, you'll do fine.

FARTHER/FURTHER

As a rule, or at least what passes for a rule, "farther" is reserved for literal physical distance ("I'm so exhausted, I can't take a step farther") and "further" is used figuratively, as a measure of degree or time ("Later this afternoon we can discuss this weighty matter further").

In the face of ambiguity, go with "further." Our friends the Brits alleviate the ambiguity by mostly using "further" for everything.

FAZE/PHASE

To faze is to bother, or to disturb, or to discompose, as someone is fazed by the prospect of speaking in public.

A phase is a stage of development, as a child may go through a phase of refusing to eat vegetables; to phase is to perform an action over time, as in phasing out outdated textbooks.

FERMENT/FOMENT

You ferment (alcoholize) beer or wine; you foment (stir up) discord. That said, your anger can ferment, and an agitated group of people can be described as being in a state of ferment.

The use of the verb "ferment" as a synonym for the verb "foment" agitates many people; it cannot, however, be said to be incorrect. Sorry, agitated people.

FICTIONAL/FICTITIOUS

"Fictional" describes the nature of works of imaginative art and the parts that make them up. The characters in a novel are fictional, as may be the towns they live in and the schools they attend.

"Fictitious" describes something not in imaginative art that is made up. The dog you don't have that ate the homework you didn't do is fictitious.

FLAIR/FLARE

The former is a knack (as, say, a flair for the dramatic) or stylishness (as someone dresses with flair); the latter is a burst of light or flame, an emergency signal, or a widening, as of nostrils.

FLAUNT/FLOUT

To flaunt is to show off: yourself or some thing. Wealth and power are popularly flaunted.

To flout is to show contempt for or to defy; the word seems to be more or less permanently attached to either "the law" or "the rules." If you flout the rules of grammar, the grammar police will come after you.

FLESH OUT/FLUSH OUT

To flesh out is to add substance, as you might flesh out a proposal for an increase in your allowance by offering substantive details of intended action.

To flush out is to clean something by forcing water through it, as a doctor might flush out a wound, or to expose something or someone by forcing it out of hiding, as you might use a smoke bomb to flush out a gang of criminals holed up in their lair. If you were in a black-and-white movie.

FLIER/FLYER

A flier is a person or thing that flies. When it comes to pieces of paper you don't want handed to you by people whose causes you're not interested in, some opt for "flier" and some for "flyer." I suggest reserving "flier" for the soaring-in-the-air thing and "flyer" for the sheet of paper heading for the recycling bin.

FLOUNDER/FOUNDER

To flounder is to struggle clumsily; to founder is to sink or to fail. Floundering may precede foundering; thus the terms are sometimes confused. It is conceivable that a flounder (the fish) could founder on a fishing hook in a pond, but why do that to a reader? Or a fish.

FOREWORD/FORWARD

A foreword is an introductory section of a book; the term is generally used to refer to a brief essay written by someone other than the book's principal author.

Forward is a direction: toward your front. It's also an adjective often applied to people who are seen as presumptuous or aggressive (often in a rude manner). Asking someone you've just met for a lick of their ice cream cone would be forward. And just plain weird.

GEL/JELL

A gel is a jelly; it is also a transparent colored sheet, usually made of plastic, used in stage lighting.

When Jell-O sets, or when your master plan takes shape, it either gels or jells. I like "jells."

GRAVELY/GRAVELLY

"Gravely" is an adverb denoting seriousness, as one may become gravely ill.

"Gravelly" is an adjective characterizing a collection of pebbles and other bits of rock, as in a gravelly road, or roughness, as in a raspy, gravelly voice. Louis Armstrong could be said to have a gravelly voice, as could Clint Eastwood and Sophia Bush (it's not a quality limited to old people—or dead people).

GRISLY/GRISTLY/GRIZZLY/GRIZZLED

Gory crimes are grisly.

Tough meat is gristly, or full of gristle.

Some bears are grizzly.

Mistaken references to "grizzly crimes" (unless committed by actual bears, in which case, sure) are alarmingly popular, always good for a chuckle, and to be avoided strenuously.

"Grizzled" refers to hair streaked with gray—and, by extension, it makes a decent synonym for "old." It does not mean, as many people seem to think it does, either unkempt or rugged.

HANGAR/HANGER

A plane parks in a hangar.

You hang your coat on a hanger.

The underappreciated cut of beef found suspended[*] from a cow's diaphragm is hanger steak.

HANGED/HUNG

Criminals used to be hanged.

Paintings are hung.

HARDY/HEARTY

Hardy people are able to cope with hardship; they are plucky, intrepid, indomitable. Resilient plants are hardy.

Hearty people have a lot of heart; they are spirited and ebullient and cheerful, often in a loud, demonstrative, and irritating fashion.

A rich, nourishing soup or stew is hearty.

---

[*] Hanging, get it?

HAWK/HOCK

Verbwise, to hawk (outside discussion of birds, that is) is to sell and to hock is to pawn.

As to loogies, you may either (traditionally) hawk them or (popularly) hock them. If you are so inclined.

HISTORIC/HISTORICAL

"Historic" denotes significance, as the passing of the Civil Rights Act was a historic event.

"Historical" simply denotes presence in the past.

Note, please: "a historic event," not "an historic event." Unless you're in the habit of saying or writing "an helicopter" or "an hydrangea," you've got no cause to say or write "an historic."

HOARD/HORDE

To hoard is to amass, often with an eye toward secrecy; that which a person hoards is their hoard. J.R.R. Tolkien's Smaug is a hoarder of gold.

"Horde" is most often used as an uncomplimentary term for a teeming crowd of something or other: Mongol invaders, say, or zombies.

HOME/HONE

Birds of prey and missiles home in on their targets.

To hone is to sharpen.

The phrase "hone in on" is one of those so-many-people-use-it-that-it-has-its-own-dictionary-entry-and-can-scarcely-anymore-be-called-an-error things, but that doesn't mean it isn't an error. Rise above it.

HUMMUS/HUMUS

Hummus is a Middle Eastern dip made from mashed chickpeas.

Humus is decaying organic matter in soil.

You will find fifty-seven varieties of hummus at your local supermarket. Try them all, except maybe the chocolate. But be careful never to eat humus.

IMPLY/INFER

To imply is to suggest, to say something without saying it.

To infer is to draw a conclusion from information perhaps obliquely offered, to figure out, to deduce.

Think of "imply" as an outward action and "infer" as an inward one. Or: Speakers imply; listeners infer.

INTERNMENT/INTERMENT

Internment is imprisoning or confining, particularly during wartime—as Japanese-Americans were interned during World War II.[*]

Interment is ritual burial, as an army guard might bury a soldier killed in action. (To put something into an urn—particularly ashes after a cremation, which I hope you don't call cremains—is to inurn it.)

IT'S/ITS

Yes, you did see this in an earlier chapter. Yes, we're going to go through it again.

"It's" is "it is," as in "It's a lovely day today."

"Its" is the possessive of "it," as in "It rubs the lotion on its skin."

An inability to discern between "its" and "it's" (and, see below, "your" and "you're") will make you a target for thunderous belittling. It's not fair, but neither is life generally.

LAY, LIE, LAID, LAIN, AND THE REST OF THE CLAN

Loath as I am to haul out the grammatical jargon, we're not going to get through the lay/lie thing without it.

---

[*] For a riveting account of what those internment camps were like, read *Farewell to Manzanar* by Jeanne Wakatsuki Houston and James D. Houston.

So: "Lay" is a transitive verb, which means that it demands an object. A transitive verb doesn't merely do; it must do *to* something. One does not merely lay; one lays a thing. I lay my hands on a long-sought volume of manga. I lay blame on a convenient stooge. I lay (if I am a hen) an egg.

What does this mean to you? Well, for a start: If you're hesitating between "lie" and "lay" and (a) your sentence has a thing to act upon and (b) you can replace the verb you're in a quandary about with a less confusingly transitive verb like "place," you need a "lay."

"Lie," on the other hand, is an intransitive verb. I lie, period. Works for both recumbence and fibbing. No object needed. "Lie" can handle an adverb (I lie down, I lie badly) or a place on which to do it (I lie on the couch); it just doesn't need a thing, a what, attached to it.

Unfortunately, both verbs can and must be conjugated, and this is where the trouble kicks in.

Let's run through them, tensely.

to lay

present	lay:	I lay the bowl on the table.
present participle	laying:	I am laying the bowl on the table.
past	laid:	Earlier, I laid the bowl on the table.
past participle	laid:	I have laid the bowl on the table.

to lie (in the sense of to recline)[*]

present	lie:	I lie down.
present participle	lying:	Look at me: I am lying down.
past	lay:	Yesterday, I lay down.
past participle	lain:	Look at me: I have lain down.

That the past participle of "lie" is "lain," which never looks right to anyone, is bad enough. That the past tense of "lie" is "lay," the very word we are trying so hard not to misuse in the first place, is maddening. I know. I'm sorry.

With practice, you may be able to commit all of these to memory. Or you may dog-ear this page and keep it handy. I know I would.

Bonus Lay/Lie Facts
The action of lying down does not require that one be a person, as some people mistakenly (and, I think, oddly) believe. I lie down. Fiona the hippopotamus lies down. Pat the bunny lies down.

You don't, in present-tense hiding, lay low or, in

---

[*] Conjugating "to lie" in the sense of to tell a whopper is pretty easy, so I'm parking it down here at the bottom of the page: I lie, I am lying, I lied, I have lied. But not to you.

ambush, lay in wait. It's "lie" all the way: I lie low; I lie in wait.

That said, you do lay a trap for your enemy, and given the chance, you will lay that enemy low.

To lay a ghost is to exorcise it.

LEAD/LED

The past tense of the verb "lead" is not "lead" but "led." Today I will lead my troops into battle; yesterday I led them.

I wouldn't point out something that seems so elementary but for the vast number of times I've seen, published, "lead" where "led" was called for. The error is not mysterious—for one thing, they sound the same; for another, compare "read," which is the past tense of "read"—but it's still an error.

LIGHTENING/LIGHTNING

If you're carrying your mother's suitcase to the train station, you are nobly lightening her load.

If on your way to the train station a thunderstorm descends, you should seek shelter, not only to stay dry but to avoid being struck by lightning.

LOATH/LOATHE

I am loath—that is, reluctant—to make comments, snide or otherwise, about people I loathe—that is, detest.

Use "loath" as an adjective; use "loathe" as a verb.

LOSE/LOOSE

To mislay something is to lose it.

Something that is not tight or severe—a dress, one's morals—is loose.

To loose something is to set it free. Oddly, to unloose something is also to set it free.

LUXURIANT/LUXURIOUS

Something lush or plentiful is luxuriant: Rapunzel's hair, say, or kudzu.

Something lavish and elegant and expensive is luxurious, like a Lamborghini or a VIP skybox at the Super Bowl.

MANTEL/MANTLE

A mantel is a shelf above a fireplace.

A mantle is a sleeveless, capelike garment. Metaphorically, it's the thing you don when you're assuming some responsibility.

MILLENNIUM/MILLENNIA

One millennium, two or more millennia. Be careful with the spelling as well: two *l*'s, two *n*'s.

In downtown Manhattan, there's a Millenium Hilton. I would never stay there.[*]

MINER/MINOR

Miners labor underground.

Minors are children.

An inconsequential detail is minor. So, musically, is a chord, scale, or key that the ear tends to associate with melancholy.

MUCOUS/MUCUS

Re "mucous," I couldn't possibly improve upon this elegant dictionary definition: "relating to, covered with, or of the nature of mucus."

That is, "mucous" is an adjective, "mucus" a noun. Mucous membranes produce mucus.

---

[*] According to a 2000 *Wired* article, whose author spoke to the hotel's public relations people, "The building's current name dates back to the early 1990s . . . when its former owner deliberately chose to spell 'Millennium' with a single *n*. . . . He was well aware that the spelling was wrong [but] figured the small aberration in nomenclature would make the hotel stand out from the crowd." Yeah, right.

NAVAL/NAVEL

People rarely err when they mean to type "naval" in the seafaring sense, but when the talk turns to belly buttons, many forget to switch from *a* to *e*. Your innie or your outie is a navel.

ONBOARD/ON BOARD

Remember "everyday" and "every day"? Well, here we are again.

"Onboard" is an adjective (onboard refueling, for instance, or an onboard navigation system); "on board" is an adverb, literally denoting presence on a vessel ("The crew was on board the ship") or figuratively denoting agreement ("This department is on board with the new regulations").

ORDINANCE/ORDNANCE

An ordinance is a decree or a piece of legislation.

"Ordnance" refers to military supplies—not only artillery but ammunition, armor, vehicles, all the practical stuff of warfare.

PALATE/PALETTE/PALLET

Your palate is the roof of your mouth or your sense of taste.

A palette is an array of color or the board onto which artists lay their paint.

A pallet is a platform onto which items are loaded, as in a warehouse; "pallet" is also a somewhat outmoded term for a small bed, usually one that's not very comfortable.

PASS/PASSED/PAST
As a verb, "passed" is the past tense of "pass."

"Past" is both noun and adjective, as in William Faulkner's "The past is never dead. It's not even past" or Shakespeare's "What's past is prologue." It's also a preposition, and an adverb, and just about anything else you can think of *except a verb*.

PEAK/PEEK/PIQUE
Mixing these up is direly easy. A peak is a summit; a peek is a glance. The *ea* in "sneak" inspires many an erroneous "sneak peak." No, please: It's "sneak peek." (Unless you find yourself jetting through a cloud and suddenly about to collide with a mountain, in which case, sure, that's a sneak peak.)

A fit of pique is a peeved little tantrum; to pique one's interest is to stimulate and excite it.

PEAL/PEEL
You probably don't need to be reminded that bells peal and potatoes are peeled. You might need to be reminded

that what you're doing when you're being watchful is keeping your eyes peeled—wide open and lids up.

The thing itself—of a potato, a banana, a lemon, an orange—is a peel. Plus—and this is why we have the verb "peel"—one removes it before eating. As opposed to a skin—an apple's, say—which outside of cooking one is apt to eat.

PEDAL/PEDDLE

You pedal a bike by pressing on its pedals. You peddle, or sell, candy/trinkets/wares. Somehow this gets past even the most experienced copy editors embarrassingly often. Let's not even throw *petal* into the mix.

PHENOMENON/PHENOMENA

As with "criterion" and "criteria" or "millennium" and "millennia" above, this is simply a matter of singular and plural: one phenomenon, two or more phenomena.

POKEY/POKY

The pokey is the hoosegow, the clink, the slammer, the big house—a prison. (Granted, it's not a term you hear much outside of black-and-white movies anymore, but a lot of those movies are worth watching, so you should file this term away.)

Something poky is irritatingly slow, or provincial, or frumpy. The Poky Little Puppy was never in jail.

In America we do the hokey pokey (and we turn ourselves around). In England they do the hokey cokey (and they turn themselves around).

POPULACE/POPULOUS

"Populace" is a noun; it means population or, particularly, the so-called common people.

"Populous" is an adjective; it means well and densely populated.

PORE/POUR

To pore over something is to examine it closely. Pores are those things on your face that get clogged.

To pour something is to tip it—water, salt, sugar, what have you—out of a container.

PRECEDE/PROCEED

To precede is to come before.

To proceed is to move forward.

PREMIER/PREMIERE

As an adjective, "premier" means first or top-ranked; as a noun, it's a head of government.

A premiere is a debut, as of a play. To premiere a movie is to open it.

PRESCRIBE/PROSCRIBE

To prescribe is to authorize medical treatment or the taking of medication, or otherwise to direct authoritatively.

To proscribe is to forbid.

PRINCIPAL/PRINCIPLE

How many times has it been explained to you in spelling lessons that "the principal is your pal"? And what was your level of disappointment when you realized that the principal is not your pal but someone charged with maintaining order even if it means giving you detention, which a pal wouldn't do?

Consider that realization a principal (that is to say, primary) life lesson. In fact, you might deem it a principle—a fundamental truth from which more advanced truths derive—on the road to critical thinking.

Your principles are your amassed moralities; villains are unprincipled.

PRONE/SUPINE

Obviously there's no confusion of vowel order or consonant doubling here, but I include these terms because they are frequently mixed up and I can't figure out where else to park them.

For the record:

To be supine is to be lying on one's back.

To be prone is to be lying on one's stomach.

Beyond "lead" when "led" is meant, I'd say that "prone" for "supine" (or vice versa) is the commonest error to get past writers, copy editors, and proofreaders and find its way to print.

You can devise all the mnemonics you like (if you're supine you're lying on your spine, if you're prone you're . . . oh, the heck with it), but I never—never—fail to consult the dictionary whenever I'm faced with either word.

PROPHECY/PROPHESY

"Prophecy" is the noun, "prophesy" the verb. An oracle prophesies a prophecy. The plural of "prophecy" is "prophecies"; the third-person singular of the verb "prophesy" is "prophesies." (I prophesy, you prophesy, he prophesies, she prophesies, they shall have prophesied, we all scream for ice cream.)

RACK/WRACK/WREAK

Setting aside the meanings pertaining to cuts of meat, the storage of clothing and spice tins, the corralling of billiard balls, and the accumulation of points, let's focus on "rack" in the sense of pain: A rack is a nasty device (we may think of it as medieval, but it has a long and distinguished history going back at least to the first century C.E.) to which one is fastened by the wrists and the ankles and, well, you know all the shrieking, limb-dislocating rest. To be put to the rack, then, is to be tortured, and thus one's body is racked with pain. One contemplates effortfully by racking one's brains. A painful cough is a racking one. And an anxiety-inducing experience is nerve-racking.

Or is it?

To wrack is to wreck, to destroy. Was that awful hour you spent locked in a room full of rambunctious kindergartners simply nerve-racking, or was it utterly nerve-wracking? Is your moldering old tree house going to wrack and ruin, or merely rack and ruin?

And what of "wreak"? To wreak is to cause (in an unnice way) or to inflict. An army wreaks havoc. A storm wreaks damage. The preferred past tense of "wreak," I should note, is not "wrought" (which is an ancient past tense of "work"; it still turns up in the phrase "wrought iron") but, simply, "wreaked."

REIGN/REIN

Monarchs reign.

Horses are reined.

If you are granted the freedom to make your own

decisions and run your own life, you are given free rein. Free rein, please, not free reign: The phrase is taken not from the devil-may-care actions of kings or queens but from permitting one's mount to do what it likes—the opposite of maintaining a tight rein. Unfortunately, "free reign" makes a kind of sense, so it's frequently—though, still, incorrectly—used.

RELUCTANT/RETICENT

To be reluctant is to be resistant, unwilling.

To be reticent is to be silent, uncommunicative.

You are reluctant to do X; you are reticent about subject Y.

"Reticent" is increasingly often used to mean "reluctant." I see no good reason to allow the distinction between these two to collapse, though many have given up on it.

RETCH/WRETCH

To retch is to heave, to gag, to nearly vomit. I think it's wonderful that the English language has a word for "to nearly vomit." (The word can also be used flat out to mean "to vomit," but there are so many other colorful synonyms for that action that surely we can leave "retch" for the preface rather than the conclusion.)

A wretch is a person on the darker side of the happiness/niceness spectrum, from the muddy gray of the deeply miserable poor unfortunate to the full-tilt blackness of the scoundrel and the miscreant. To say nothing of the blackguard.

RIFFLE/RIFLE

This duo plays well to the onomatopoeia/mnemonics crowd, because to riffle something is to thumb lightly through it, as, say, through the pages of a book or a deck of playing cards, and the word "riffle," at least to my ears, has that lovely susurrating sound built right into it. To rifle through something—a room, a desk drawer—is to rummage with criminal intent to steal. That the verb "rifle" is the same as a noun for a firearm should also make it easier for you to remember which one of these is which.

SEGUE/SEGWAY

The music-derived "segue" means, as a verb, to transition seamlessly and, as a noun, such a seamless transition. Before the invention of the motorized two-wheeled Segway, "segue" was, lacking a homophone, likely never misspelled. Now it is. A lot. A smooth change is not a "segway." Ever.

SHONE/SHOWN

"Shone" is the past and past participle of shine (so is "shined," if you like "shined," or if you're using "shine" as a transitive verb: The detective shined the flashlight on the crime scene). "Shown" is the past participle of "show."

STANCH/STAUNCH

These two derive from a single root, and each is occasionally offered as a synonym for the other, but if you're, as I perennially am, in a compartmentalizing mood:

Use "stanch" when you mean to stop the flow of something, as blood from a wound, or to hold something in check, as to stanch the rising violence in a war-torn country.

And use "staunch" to describe someone who is indomitable, steadfast, loyal, and strong. Britain is a staunch ally of the United States.

STATIONARY/STATIONERY

To be stationary is to be unmoving.

Stationery is writing paper (and, often included in the idea, the full array of envelopes, pens, pencils, and ink). There are approximately three convenience store awnings in New York City on which "stationery" is spelled correctly. And they probably don't sell stationery anymore.

THAN/THEN

Beyond mixing these up with a slip of the fingers, many people mix them up syntactically when they mistype

"No sooner had we placed our order with the waiter *then* the restaurant caught on fire" when they should be adhering to the correct construction "no sooner had x *than* y."

THEIR/THERE/THEY'RE

I told you you'd see this again.

"Their" is a possessive meaning belongs to them: I can see their house from here.

"There" is a direction indicating a place that is not here: I can see their house, which is over there.

"They're" is a contraction for "they are": They're walking to their house.

As with "it's/its" (above), "to/too" (below), and "your/you're" (yet farther below), you simply need to get this right. It's not enough to know the differences; you must also apply them.

TO/TOO

I know I shouldn't have to clear this up, but you'd be saddened to learn how frequently even adults get it wrong.

"To" is, among many things, a preposition, as in "He walked to the store"; what is called an infinitive marker, as in the verb "to be"; and an occasional adverb, as in "She yanked the door to"—which is to say, she pulled it shut—or "He came to"—meaning he became conscious.

"Too" means also (as in "eating one's cake and having it too") and excessively (as in "Slow down, you move too fast").

TORTUOUS/TORTUROUS

The former means twisty, winding, serpentine; the latter means like torture. A tortuous journey can be torturous, but there is no judgment inherent in "tortuous"; it's merely descriptive. "Torturous," no matter how you slice it, or are sliced by it, is unpleasant.

UNDERWAY/UNDER WAY

As above, with "everyday" and "every day" and "onboard" and "on board," "underway" is an adjective, "under way" an adverb. You won't have much (or any) use of the former, so odds are you want the latter. The voyage is under way, the project is under way, your life is under way. More and more lately, "underway" is used as an adverb. Bummer, I say.

VALE/VEIL

A vale is a valley; a veil is a face covering.

As picturesquely funereally evocative as the notion of a "veil of tears" might be, the phrase—going all the way back to Psalm 84—is properly "vale of tears."

WAIVE/WAVE/WAVER

To waive is to renounce or cede, as one waives one's right to a trial by jury.

To wave is to flap one's hand about (or to curl one's hair).

A customs inspector who lets you pass without examining your luggage is waving—not waiving—you through.

To waver (not to be confused with a waiver, which is a document of relinquishment) is to tremble or to vacillate.

WHOSE/WHO'S

"I don't know whose books those are." "Whose" is a pronoun denoting belonging.

"Who's on first?" "Who's" means "Who is."

WORKOUT/WORK OUT

The former is a noun; the latter is a verb. You're not on the way to the gym to "workout." You're on the way to the gym to work out. And to give yourself a workout.

YOUR/YOU'RE

This should be old hat by now.

Just like "whose" and "who's." "This is not your book but one stolen from the library. You're in a world of trouble."

CHAPTER 9

NOTES ON PROPER NOUNS

I think I can safely say that no rational person is confident enough to type "Quvenzhané Wallis" or "Thandiwe Abdullah" or "Saoirse Ronan" without first checking the spelling of the name, but the number of proper nouns that wind up misspelled in manuscripts and, if copy editors and proofreaders are not vigilant, in finished books, is vast. In response to a few near misses and a few published oopses, I began keeping this list years ago; in fact, it's the germ of the book you're now reading, and I have a great sentimental attachment to it. And I can't stop adding things to it.[*]

I suppose I might just say "If it starts with a capital

---

[*] The list, you'll note, leans heavily toward the performing arts. As Popeye once said: I yam what I yam. Also, I've found over time that many writers about the performing arts are irksomely cavalier about spelling. And dates.

letter, look it up" and end this chapter right here, but where would be the fun in that?

People*

HANS CHRISTIAN ANDERSEN
Writer of fairy tales such as "The Little Mermaid" and "The Ugly Duckling." The international Hans Christian Andersen Award is given every other year to authors and illustrators of children's books.
    Not "Anderson."

ATTILA
Hun. Ruthless king of a vast empire in the fifth century C.E.
    Not "Atilla."

ELIZABETH BENNET
Headstrong heroine of Jane Austen's *Pride and Prejudice*.
    Just the one *t* in Bennet.
    It's not "Jane Austin." Does that bear mentioning? I fear that it does.

---

* Also a fairy, a bear, and a few other beings that can't quite be called people.

GAUTAMA BUDDHA
Aka Siddhartha Gautama, aka the Buddha.
> Sage.
> Not "the Bhudda."
> Also, then, not "Bhuddist" but "Buddhist."

JULIUS CAESAR
Roman emperor after whom caesarean delivery was likely not named.
> Not "Ceasar."
> The salad—born, untraumatically, not in Rome but in Mexico—is also Caesar.
> The activist Chavez (activist) and the entertainer Romero (who played the Joker in the classic 1960s *Batman* show), among many others, were Cesars.

NICOLAS CAGE
Film actor.
> Not "Nicholas."
> Nephew of film director Francis Ford Coppola and cousin of FFC's daughter, film director Sofia Coppola, whose surname is occasionally misspelled "Copolla." (Italian words with double consonants seem to confound people; be on your guard.)

ROSANNE CASH
Singer/songwriter/writing writer.
   Most definitely not "Roseanne."

HILLARY RODHAM CLINTON
Politician; nearly our nation's first woman president. A two-*l* Hillary.
   Novelist Mantel and actress Swank are one-*l* Hilarys.

E. E. CUMMINGS
Edward Estlin Cummings, in full. Poet.
   His name is not "e. e. cummings."[*]

A Note on Initials
Random House (my employer) style[†] favors even spacing overall for names featuring two initials; that is:

---

[*] Though in styling his name publishers and text designers occasionally mimicked Cummings's penchant for writing all in lowercase by styling his name "e. e. cummings," the writer himself far more often than not favored standard capitalization insofar as his name was concerned.

[†] Every publishing house has its own style, called, aptly enough, house style, which is usually determined by the head of the copyediting and/or editorial department. It comprises a conglomeration of select stylebooks, dictionaries, exceptions to rules, pet peeves, and prohibitions, and woe betide you should you fail to conform.

E. E. Cummings (rather than E.E. Cummings)

T. S. Eliot (rather than T.S. Eliot)

H. L. Mencken (you get the point)

to say nothing of

George R. R. Martin

For names featuring three initials, go with the more compact

J.R.R. Tolkien

for instance, because on the page, J. R. R. Tolkien, not unlike the Peter Jackson films taken from his books, goes on for bloody ever.

More and more often I'm seeing, for people who truly use their initials as a first name, such stylings as

PJ Harvey

and

KT Tunstall

which I think look spiffy and make good sense, an enviably fine combination.

Mostly you want to strike a balance between editorial preferences and the preferences of the people who own the names.

CRUELLA DE VIL

Puppy-coat-craving archvillainess.

Not "de Ville," as I often encounter it.

While we're here: Dodie Smith's 1956 novel is *The Hundred and One Dalmatians*. The 1961 Disney animated film thereof was first released as *One Hundred and One Dalmatians;* it's now generally marketed as *101 Dalmatians,* which is the official title of the 1996 live-action remake.

The spotted dogs are not "Dalmations," though that error attempts to happen every so often.

W.E.B. DU BOIS

Writer and civil rights activist.

His surname is correctly rendered "Du Bois" and not (as for Tennessee Williams's Blanche, in the play *A Streetcar Named Desire*) "DuBois."

And it's pronounced not "doo-BWAH" (which would be correct for Williams's Blanche) but "doo-BOYZ."

T. S. ELIOT

Poet, and person ultimately responsible for the musical *Cats*.

This is your reminder always to look up Eliots, Elyots, Elliots, and Elliotts.

MAHATMA GANDHI

Nonviolent revolutionary.

Born Mohandas Karamchand Gandhi.

"Mahatma," by the way, isn't a name per se. It's a Sanskrit honorific, meaning "great soul."

All that taken into account, the surname is not "Ghandi," as it's misspelled with dismaying frequency.

THEODOR GEISEL

Aka Dr. Seuss.

Cat in the Hat creator.

Not a Theodore with a second *e*. [*]

ALLEN GINSBERG

Poet of the Beat Generation, young artists in the 1940s and 1950s who challenged literary convention.

Always verify the name of anyone who is named Allen, Allan, Alan, Ginsberg, Ginsburg (Ruth Bader, for instance), or even Ginzburg.

JAKE GYLLENHAAL

Actor.

---

[*] Whenever you're about to write something like "Not a Theodore with an *e*," as I was just about to, make your way back to the beginning of the word, count up your letters, and adjust your math accordingly.

Also, for that matter, Maggie Gyllenhaal, his sister. Actress.

George Frideric Handel

Composer of the late Baroque era.

This, above, is his own anglicized version of his name; in the original German he's Georg Friedrich Händel.

O. Henry

Pen name of twisty-ending-short-story writer William Sydney Porter, author of "The Gift of the Magi," every English teacher's go-to example of irony.

Not "O'Henry."

The candy bar is Oh Henry!; it was not, as many people think, named after baseball player Henry Louis "Hank" Aaron.

Katharine Hepburn

Radiant personality and occasionally brilliant actress.

Not "Katherine."

Adolf Hitler

Genocidal maniac democratically elected to run an ostensibly enlightened nation.

It's not "Adolph."

SCARLETT JOHANSSON
Actress.

Two *t*'s in Scarlett, like in Scarlett O'Hara.

NIKITA KHRUSHCHEV
Premier of the former Soviet Union and shoe banger.*

You'd think that people would always look up a tricky name like Khrushchev. You'd be wrong.

FREDDY KRUEGER
Frequenter of Elm Street.

Not "Kreuger." And not "Kruger." And not "Kroger."

SHIA LABEOUF
Star of *Holes,* the film adaptation of Louis Sachar's beloved book of the same name. I appreciate people who take the time to spell this odd actor's odd name correctly. In a more sensible French-cognizant world, it would be spelled LeBoeuf.

LEONARDO DA VINCI
Quite literally, Renaissance man.

He's set here between LaBeouf and Lévi-Strauss rather

---

* Legend has it that Khrushchev became so angry at a United Nations meeting in New York in 1960 that he removed one of his shoes and banged it on the table in protest.

than up among the *D*'s because his name is, indeed, Leonardo and he shouldn't be referred to as "Da Vinci." Vinci is the town in Italy he was from; it's not his name. That novel by Dan Brown has done much to blunt this particular point, but getting this right remains a laudable thing to do.

CLAUDE LÉVI-STRAUSS

Anthropologist.

(The unrelated company that makes the jeans is Levi Strauss.)

ROY LICHTENSTEIN

Pop artist.

I occasionally see the spelling of his name confused with that of the little landlocked European country hemmed in by Switzerland and Austria, which are themselves landlocked, and which is the Principality of Liechtenstein.

MACBETH

Shakespeare's thane of Cawdor.

Not "MacBeth."

It's the wise writer who looks up any name starting with Mac- or Mc-, whether it belongs to an apple (McIntosh) or to a computer (Macintosh), or to James Abbott McNeill Whistler (painter), Fred MacMurray (actor), or Old MacDonald (farmer).

While we're here: The theatrical superstition against uttering the name Macbeth is often misrepresented. You may safely utter it, say, walking down Forty-Fourth Street in New York City, or at dinner. Or while reading this book aloud. You may not utter it, except during rehearsals or performances, in a theater. Thus the euphemisms "the Scottish play," "the Scottish lord," etc.

MATTHEW MCCONAUGHEY
Actor.
His surname is impossible to spell correctly.

IAN MCKELLEN
Actor. Gandalf in the Lord of the Rings films by Peter Jackson.
His name is—inexplicably, I'd say; one might just as easily get it right as get it wrong—often misrendered "McKellan."

STEPHENIE MEYER
Writer of the Twilight series.
Not "Stephanie."

FRIEDRICH WILHELM NIETZSCHE
Trouble-causing German philosopher.
There are, I've learned over the years, so many, many ways to misspell Nietzsche.

GEORGIA O'KEEFFE
Artist.

Two *f*'s.

EDGAR ALLAN POE
Writer.

I'd venture to say that Poe's is the most consistently misspelled author's name in the so-called Western canon. His central name is not "Allen."

SPIDER-MAN
Superhero.

Note the hyphen, note the capital *M*.

MOTHER TERESA
Nun, missionary, now a Catholic saint.

Not Theresa.

TINKER BELL
Fairy.

Two words, "bell" conveying the sound of her communication, "tinker" conveying that her job was to mend pots and pans. Really.

HARRY S. TRUMAN

President on whose desk was a sign reading THE BUCK STOPS HERE, meaning "I am ultimately the one to blame." Truman was responsible for dropping both atomic bombs on Japan to end World War II.

The middle initial doesn't stand for anything, so for decades copy editors have amused themselves, if no one else, by styling his name as Harry S Truman. Truman seems to have (mostly) signed his name with a perioded *S,* so let's do it that way.

WINNIE-THE-POOH
Bear.

A. A. Milne styled the bear's full name with hyphens (though the character is also called, hyphenlessly, Pooh Bear). The Disney folk do not.

Places

ANTARCTICA
One of the seven continents, situated around the South Pole. Two *c*'s.

ARCTIC
Relating to the North Pole or the area near it. I know; it's confusing. Also two *c*'s.

CINCINNATI
City in Ohio. Not "Cincinatti."

COLOMBIA
South American country. Two *o*'s.

Columbia, with a *u,* is, among other things, a New York university, a recording company, a Hollywood movie studio, the District also known as Washington, the Gem of the Ocean (as in that old patriotic song) and the female representation of the United States.

GRAND CENTRAL TERMINAL
Magnificent Beaux Arts structure located at the junction of Forty-Second Street and Park Avenue in New York City—a junction and not an intersection because the streets meet but do not cross.

That the building is often referred to as Grand Central Station does not make that its name. That said, if you're going to characterize a busy and/or crowded place by saying "It's like Grand Central Station in here!," you should go ahead and do that because that's what everyone does, and there are occasions when idiom outweighs* accuracy.

---

* I'd originally written here "idiom trumps accuracy," but I've developed an aversion to that verb.

MISSISSIPPI
Some people, myself included, can't ever spell it correctly without singing the 1916 song that still popped up in elementary school music classes when I was a tot (much later than 1916). Do you know it too?

ROMANIA
The spellings Roumania and Rumania are obsolete.

TUCSON, ARIZONA
Not "Tuscon."

Other Bits and Pieces of Social, Cultural, and Historical Arcana That Turn Up, with Reasonable Frequency, Often Misrendered

---

ALICE'S ADVENTURES IN WONDERLAND
The full title of Lewis Carroll's 1865 deceptively lighthearted fantasy,* though it cannot be denied that people have been calling it *Alice in Wonderland* pretty much since it was published. The 1871 sequel is *Through the Looking-Glass, and What Alice Found There.* You may

---

* I'd suggest avoiding the "deceptively [adjective] [thing]" construction entirely, because it's often impossible to tell whether a deceptively [adjective] [thing] is extremely that [adjective] or entirely not that [adjective]. What's a deceptively large room, for instance?

drop the second half of that title; don't drop the hyphen in "Looking-Glass."

BULFINCH'S MYTHOLOGY

Classic book of Greek mythology written by single-*l* Thomas Bulfinch, not by a double-*l* bird.

THE DIARY OF A YOUNG GIRL

The title under which Anne Frank's journal was first published in English.

The Diary of Anne Frank is the title of a play by Frances Goodrich and Albert Hackett, as well as of its film adaptations.

FRANKENSTEIN

The title of the novel by Mary Shelley (in full: *Frankenstein; or, The Modern Prometheus*). Also the title of (among other adaptations) the 1931 Universal film directed by James Whale and starring Boris Karloff.

Though confusion between the two commenced almost immediately upon the novel's publication, Frankenstein is not the name of the man-made man concocted and brought to life by scientist Victor Frankenstein (Henry Frankenstein in the Karloff film and its immediate sequels) from dead tissue secured in "charnel-houses . . . the dissecting room and the slaughter-house."

Shelley calls him, among other things, "creature," "monster," "vile insect" (that's a good one), and "daemon." The 1931 film bills him, simply, as "The Monster."

It's not OK to call Frankenstein's monster "Frankenstein," and people who willfully advocate for this make me cross.

JEOPARDY!

The game show. With an exclamation point!

THE JUILLIARD SCHOOL

Prestigious performing arts conservatory in New York City. You learn to spell it correctly the same way you get to nearby Carnegie Hall: Practice.

LOVE'S LABOUR'S LOST

Shakespeare comedy. Americanizing out the *u* in *Labour's* is disrespectful; omitting either apostrophe is just plain wrong.

MOBY-DICK; OR, THE WHALE

Much confusion swirls around that hyphen, which in the original 1851 publication of Herman Melville's novel appeared on the title page but nowhere else. If you hyphenate the novel's title and otherwise leave the whale's name open as Moby Dick, you'll be safe. That said, just about every film adaptation I can track drops the hyphen entirely.

OKLAHOMA!

The exclamation mark in the title of this Rodgers and Hammerstein musical should not be neglected, nor should the exclamation marks in *Hello, Dolly!*; *Mamma Mia!*; *Oliver!*; *Piff! Paff!! Pouf!!!*; and similarly excitable Broadway shows.

"OVER THE RAINBOW"

The song MGM head honcho Louis B. Mayer wanted cut from *The Wizard of Oz* because he thought it was slowing the picture down.

The "somewhere" is in the lyric; it's not in the title.

THE PICTURE OF DORIAN GRAY

The eminently quotable[*] novel by the eminently quotable Oscar Wilde.

Not "Portrait."

Not "Grey."

---

[*] "There is no such thing as a moral or an immoral book. Books are well written, or badly written. That is all." Even for the epigrammatically adept Wilde, that's spectacular.

REVELATION
The New Testament's Book of Revelation, also known as the Apocalypse.

Not "Revelations."

THE WONDERFUL WIZARD OF OZ
The full title of L. Frank Baum's 1900 cyclonic fantasy novel.

Gale, the surname of the story's heroine, Dorothy, is not given in Baum's first Oz novel or in *The Marvelous Land of Oz,* its superb sequel, though it turns up in later volumes. It debuted in a 1902 Broadway musical in which, perhaps because little dogs are intractable and hard to see in a large theater, a cow named Imogene was subbed in for the beloved Toto.

No, not a real cow. Don't be silly.

WOOKIEE
Everyone gets it wrong. It's not "Wookie."

Also on the subject of the world of Star Wars, "lightsaber" is one word, "dark side" is lowercased (oddly enough), and "A long time ago in a galaxy far, far away. . . ." ends with a period and three ellipsis points, even though it is not a complete sentence, because that's how the Star Wars people like it. And if you challenge them on any of these points, they'll cut your hand off. True story.

CHAPTER 10

THE TRIMMABLES

There's a lot of deleting in copyediting, not just of the "very"s and "rather"s and "quite"s and "that"s with which we all encase our prose like so much Bubble Wrap and packing peanuts, but of restatements of information—"AS ESTAB'D," I might politely write in the margin to point out that yes, we know already.

Much repetition, though, comes under the more elementary heading of Two Words Where One Will Do, or redundancies. Some of the following may strike you as obvious—though their obviousness doesn't stop them from showing up constantly. Others are the sorts of things you could likely get away with without anyone's noticing—but they're snippable nonetheless.

(The bits in italics are the bits you can dispose of.)

absolutely certain, *absolute* certainty, *absolutely* essential

added bonus

advance planning, *advance* warning

all-time record
As well, you don't set a "new record." You merely set a record.

ATM *machine*
ATM = automated teller machine, which, you might argue and win the argument, is redundant enough as it is.

blend *together*

cameo *appearance,* cameo *role*

capitol *building*

closed fist
A closed hand is, I suppose, a thing. But as there are no open fists, neither are there closed ones.

close proximity
Like "from whence" (see below), "close proximity" can be defended simply by its lengthy history of turning up

in competent prose, but to be proximate is, inarguably, to be close, so if you need to emphasize intimacy, perhaps find a less galumphing way to do it.

CNN *network*
CNN = Cable News Network.

consensus *of opinion, general* consensus
The word "consensus" has the "general" and the "of opinion" baked right in. It doesn't need any help.

continue *on*
The airlines like it. I don't.

crisis *situation*

depreciated *in value*

direct confrontation

disappear *from sight*

earlier *in time*

end product

end result

I can appreciate the difference between a midprogress result and an ultimate result, but "end result" is cloddish.

equally as, equally *as*

Use one or the other, not both. Alan Jay Lerner's "I'd be equally as willing for a dentist to be drilling / than to ever let a woman in my life," from *My Fair Lady,* is often pointed out by aficionados as one of the prime grammatical calamities in musical theater lyric writing—not only the "equally as" but that "than" that should certainly be an "as." That the singer of the lyric is the persnickety grammarian Henry Higgins only adds to the ironic fun.

exact same

To be sure, "exact same" is redundant. To be sure, I still say it and write it.

fall *down*

What are you going to do, fall up?

fellow countryman

few *in number*

fiction novel
Appalling. A novel is a work of fiction. That's why it's called a novel.

Lately one encounters people referring to any full-length book, even a work of nonfiction, as a novel. That has to stop.

final outcome

follow *after*

free gift
A classic of the redundancy genre, much beloved of retailers and advertisers.

from whence
Whence means "from where," which makes "from whence" redundant. Still, the phrase has a lot of history, including, from the King James Version of the Bible, "I will lift up mine eyes unto the hills, from whence cometh my help." So I suppose you can write "from whence" if you're also talking about thine eyes and the place your help is cometh from.

full gamut
A gamut is the full range or scope of something, so the word needs no modifier. Ditto "complete range," "broad spectrum," "full extent," and their cousins.

fuse *together*

future plans

gather *together*
Yes, I know: "We Gather Together (to Ask the Lord's Blessing)" and "For where two or three are gathered together in my name, there am I in the midst of them" (Matthew 18:20). Two wrongs, even sacred ones, do not make a divine right. We can just gather.

glance *briefly*
Indeed, that's what your garden-variety glance is: a brief look (or quick or momentary).

HIV *virus*
HIV = human immunodeficiency virus.

hollow tube
Bet you hadn't thought of that one, had you.

hourly (or daily or weekly or monthly or yearly) *basis*

integrate *with each other*

interdependent *upon each other*

join *together*

kneel *down*

last *of all*

lift *up*

main protagonist
I don't hold with the notion that a story can have no more than one protagonist, but "main protagonist" grates.

merge *together*

might *possibly*

moment *in time*
Whitney Houston notwithstanding.

more superior

mutual cooperation

___ o'clock A.M. *in the morning*
Just plain unacceptable. Ditto "P.M. at night."
    While we're here, let's dispatch "twelve midnight" and "twelve noon"; "midnight" and "noon" are all you need to say.

orbit *around*

*over*exaggerate
Even spellcheck sneers at it.

passing fad
A fad is, by definition, of brief duration. A fancy may not be (though it's certainly superficial and usually capricious), so Ira Gershwin ("The radio and the telephone / and the movies that we know / may just be passing fancies and in time may go") and Cole Porter ("And it's not a passing fancy or a fancy pass") are in the clear.

past history
Also *past* experience. If you use this as a header on your résumé, you're sabotaging yourself.

personal friend, *personal* opinion

"Personal," more often than not, begs to be deleted whenever or wherever it shows up.* And the only thing worse than "my personal opinion" is "my own personal opinion."

plan *ahead*

*pre*plan

Horrid.†

raise *up*

reason *why*

I include this here largely to disinclude it. You can usually do without the "why," but there's no particular reason you ought. Not "the reason is because," though. That's a bit much.

---

* I'd like to be able to condemn "personal friend" as a product of our modern era of actual friends and virtual friends, but I can't, as I've found numerous uses of the phrase going back to the 1800s.

† An awful lot of "pre-" compounds work just fine without the prefix, so be on your guard. Some people quibble over "preorder," but it does carry a meaning that "order" doesn't quite: If I order something, I expect it to be delivered as close to immediately as is humanly possible. If I preorder something—a book, say—I recognize that it's not yet available and that I'm going to have to wait for it.

regular routine

return (or recall or revert or many other things beginning with "re-") *back*

rise *up*
If you think I'm going to pick a fight with Lin-Manuel
Miranda, who uses the phrase "rise up" repeatedly in
Hamilton's "My Shot," you have another think coming.

shuttle *back and forth*

sink *down*

skirt *around*

slightly ajar

sudden impulse

surrounded *on all sides*

swoop *down*
To be nitpickingly technical about it, swooping is a
downward action, so "swoop down" is one more word
than one needs. But everyone says it, so let's give it a

pass. We're also very used to "swoop up," as in swooping up (or scooping up) a dropped ball or child.

unexpected surprise
Dreadful. And common, in both senses of the word.

unsolved mystery
Once it's solved, it's not a mystery anymore, is it.

usual custom

wall mural
No, really, I've seen this.

Copyediting FAQ
Q. What's the most redundant redundancy you've ever encountered?

A. I recall it as if it were yesterday:

"He implied without quite saying."

I was so filled with delight on encountering that, I scarcely had the heart to cross out "without quite saying" and to note in the margin, politely and succinctly, "BY DEF" (i.e., by definition).

But I did it anyway.

CHAPTER 11

THE MISCELLANY

Here's everything I can think of that I think is important—or at least interesting, or at least simply odd—that I couldn't find a place for elsewhere.

1.
Strictly differentiating between "each other," in reference to something occurring between two people,

> Johnny and I like each other.

and "one another," for three or more,

> "Everybody get together, try to love one another right now."

is yet another of those shakily justifiable rules invented by some obscure grammarian of centuries past that, nonetheless, I like to observe, particularly as many writers flip back and forth between the two apparently at random, and randomness in writing, unlike raindrops on roses and whiskers on kittens, is not one of my favorite things. You cannot properly be criticized if you don't follow the rule (or, let's say, "rule"), but neither can you be criticized if you do.

2.

You'll hear a lot of people say things like this: "If I would have known she was sick, I would have stayed away." "If she would have just told me, I would have invited her along." Please, please don't be one of those people. The verb mood used here should be the subjunctive, in the past tense: "If I had known she was sick" and "If she had just told me." Getting this wrong is, in my opinion, one of the most telling reflections of your regard—or lack thereof—for language.

3.

If you only see one movie this year . . .

Normal human beings frontload the word "only" at the beginning of a sentence. Copy editors will tend to pick up that "only" and drop it next to the thing that's being "only"d:

If you see only one movie this year . . .

Or, for instance:

NORMAL HUMAN BEING: You can only watch a
movie ironically so many times before you're
watching it earnestly.
COPY EDITOR: You can watch a movie ironically
only so many times before you're watching it
earnestly.

Does the latter perhaps sound a bit stilted? Maybe,
but to be perfectly honest, there's a certain tautness in
slightly stilted prose that I find almost viscerally thrilling.

I also think that readers don't much notice when
prose is wound up a bit too tight but may well, and not
favorably, notice overloose prose.

Moreover, a loosely placed "only" can distort the
meaning of a sentence entirely.

That said, in fiction, especially fiction with an informal
narrative voice and, even more so, dialogue in fiction, I'm
most likely to leave the "only" where the author set it.*

---

* This also applies to the temporal use of "just" and the difference between
writing, say, "I almost just tripped on the stairs," which sounds perfectly
natural, and "I just almost tripped on the stairs," which makes a bit more
sense. If I've inspired you to give it an extra thought every time you're
about to write or say the words "only" and "just," I feel I've done my job.

4.

Fifty-eight years and counting after the assassination of John F. Kennedy and the conspiracy theories it gave birth to, I continue to caution writers against describing any other grassy knoll besides the mysterious grassy knoll in Dallas, Texas, as a "grassy knoll." It remains, I think, a distractingly potent term.

5.

Here's a fun weird thing: The word "namesake" works in both directions. That is, if you were named after your grandfather, you are his namesake. He is also yours. Who knew.

6.

Clichés should be avoided like the plague.

7.

There's a world of difference between going into the water (an action generally accompanied by flailing and shrieking and other merriment) and going in the water (an action generally accompanied by staring abstractedly into the distance, and, no, you're not fooling anyone), and it's a difference to be honored.

Into = movement.

In = presence.

The same applies to, say, "jumping into a lake" (transferring from pier to water) and "jumping in a lake" (in the water already and propelling oneself vertically upward), but the vernacular being what it is, no one will object to the traditional dismissal "Aww, go jump in a lake."

8.
There's also a world of difference between turning in to a driveway, which is a natural thing to do with one's car, and turning into a driveway, which is a Merlyn trick.

9.
Of two brothers, one fifteen and one seventeen, the fifteen-year-old is the younger, not the youngest, and the seventeen-year-old is the older (or elder, if you like), not the oldest (or eldest).

It takes three to make an "-est."

Except, English being English, in the phrase "best foot forward."

10.
If you love something passionately and vigorously, you love it no end. To love something "to no end," as one often sees it rendered, would be to love it pointlessly. If that's what you mean, then OK.

II.

The habit of inauthentically attributing wisecracks, purported profundities, inspirational doggerel, and other bits of refrigerator-door wisdom to famous people is scarcely new—members of the press, particularly newspaper columnists, have been doing it for decades—but the internet has grossly exacerbated the problem, with numerous quote-aggregation sites irresponsibly devoted to prettily packaging the fakery, thus encouraging the unwary (or uncaring) to snarf it up, then hork it up, ad nauseam.

To cite one majestically apposite instance: In July 2017, the writer Colin Dickey stumbled upon a 2013 tweet from the elder daughter of the person who would, eventually, assume the presidency of the United States:

> If the facts don't fit the theory, change the facts.
>
> —ALBERT EINSTEIN

As Dickey then himself tweeted, "That Einstein never said any such thing only makes this tweet that much more perfect."

And indeed and in fact, and no matter the hundreds of Google hits suggesting otherwise, the quip never emerged from the mouth or pen of Albert Einstein. It's

simply a bit of unattributable pseudo-cleverness as-
signed, presumably to lend it weightiness and importance, to someone who, particularly in this case, would
never have said it.

Einstein is only one of the pin-the-wisdom-on-the-
maven targets. Five'll get you ten that a quote you find
attributed, particularly without reference to a published
source, to Abraham Lincoln is inauthentic; the same goes
for Mark Twain, Oscar Wilde (and with the thousands of
witticisms Wilde uttered, why would anyone put words
into his mouth?), Winston Churchill, and Dorothy Parker
(like Wilde, an industrial-strength generator of cleverness).*

There are any number of ways to verify or debunk
quotes:

- Wikiquote, with individual entries for
  just about everyone who ever picked up a
  pen, not only lists a writer's greatest hits
  but helpfully links you to the published
  sources of said hits and, perhaps even more
  helpfully, includes reliable sections on
  disputed and misattributed quotes.

---

* Also, in no particular order, Ralph Waldo Emerson, Henry David
Thoreau, Voltaire, Mahatma Gandhi, and (impudently and absurdly, given
how easily traceable every word he ever wrote is) William Shakespeare.

- If you want to explore on your own, make use of the highly searchable books.google .com. If you can't, with a modicum of effort, find a published source for a quote, the odds are at least reasonable that it's a sham.
- I also commend to you the work of the doggedly thorough Garson O'Toole, who runs the Quote Investigator website (quoteinvestigator.com) and tweets as @QuoteResearch, and who specializes in not only debunking fake or misattributed quotes but time-traveling through the archives to discern, if he can, how and when the fakeries and misattributions first occurred.

Now, what has any of this to do with writing?

Lazy writers often litter their manuscripts with allegedly uplifting epigraphs they've plucked from either the internet or the works of their equally lazy predecessors, and thus the manure gets spread.

I beg you not to perpetrate and perpetuate these fortune-cookie hoaxes, which are often empty words and are as demeaning to the spirit as in their inauthenticity they are insulting to the history of the written word.

May I make a suggestion?

Build yourself, on either a virtual or a paper tablet, what's known as a commonplace book—someplace you can copy down bits of writing you find clever and/or meaningful—and keep it handy for future use, even if that future use is simply your own edification. (Don't forget to make note of where you found the stuff.) Then, if you ever find yourself in a position to share with the world your own wisdom and want to periodically sprinkle it with others' smarts, you'll at least have something fresh and heartfelt to offer.

12.

Q. What do you have to say about the increasing use of "woman" as an adjective, rather than "female," as in "woman candidate" instead of "female candidate"? It's not as if anyone ever says "man candidate."

A. People don't often say "male candidate," either; they just say "candidate." I suppose that brevity goes back to the peculiar notion that a default human being is a male.* Or a man. I, like you, do increasingly see

---

* At the dawn of my career I frequently encountered in manuscripts the unspoken notion that a default human being was white. That is, only nonwhite characters would ever have their race specifically called out. You'll still often run into the idea that the unmodified use of "man"—as in articles about what men do or don't like about women—inarguably means "heterosexual man." It doesn't.

"woman" used as an adjective; I wonder if it's because to some people the word "female" looks particularly biological, as if a "female cashier," say, totes up your purchases with her uterus. That said, the use of "woman" as an adjective isn't particularly new. You want to be especially careful, though, not to turn the tables and refer to a woman as "a female." "Female" as a noun is rarely meant as a compliment, and it's unlikely to be taken as one.

And, I must emphasize: *Whether* you choose to characterize people by gender is not my business. *How* you do it is.

13.

A button-down shirt is a shirt whose collar points fasten to buttons on the upper-chestal zone of the shirt. It is not any old shirt that buttons from neck to waist. Call that a dress shirt, if it happens to be one. Or a button-up shirt, which is both accurate and, in the context, amusing.

14.

You don't tow the line. You toe it.

15.

The approving exclamation is not "Here, here!" but "Hear, hear!"

16.

Something that is well established down to the marrow is not "deep-seeded," which may sound as if it makes sense but, I'm assured by people who know how plants work, doesn't. It is, rather, "deep-seated."

17.

In an emergency you call 911.

The similarly numbered day of catastrophe was 9/11. (In the rest of the world it's 11/9, but we Americans are alarmingly stubborn in our date styling.)

18.

A reversal is a total 180.* If you do a total 360, you're facing the same direction as when you began.

19.

I note that, increasingly often, some people refer to other people referring to themselves as "we" as "speaking in the second person." Nope. Speaking of oneself as "we"— which unless you're Queen Victoria you oughtn't—is speaking in the first person plural. The second person is "you," as in, as a writer once wrote, "You are not the

---

* Is the term "full 180" redundant? Isn't it enough to say "I did a 180"? Sure, and sure. And yet.

kind of guy who would be at a place like this at this time of morning."

20.

The line from *Hamlet* is not "Methinks the lady doth protest too much"; it's "The lady doth protest too much, methinks." Also, if you haven't been dead for four hundred years and are planning on using the word "methinks" in the spirit of roguish cleverness, please don't.

21.

They're not Brussel sprouts. They're Brussels sprouts.

OK, I'm done.

OUTRO

BY WAY OF CONCLUSION

I think perhaps you don't finish writing a book. You stop writing it.

My favorite last line in all literature has long been this, from Virginia Woolf's *To the Lighthouse*:

> It was done; it was finished. Yes, she thought, laying down her brush in extreme fatigue, I have had my vision.

I lack, by far, Lily Briscoe's certainty, though I recognize her exhaustion.

An early title for this book was *The Last Word*, which was soon discarded for any number of excellent reasons, one of them being that there is no last word.

There's no rule without an exception (well, mostly), there's no thought without an afterthought (at least for me), there's always something you meant to say but forgot to say.

There's no last word, only the next word.

THINGS I LIKE

Beyond the sources of information already mentioned throughout, I commend to you:

Theodore Bernstein's *Miss Thistlebottom's Hobgoblins,* one of the charmingest, smartest, most readable books on the subject of language I've ever read

and these exceptionally erudite, eminently bookmarkable sites, to which I return over and over:

Grammarist (grammarist.com)
Patricia T. O'Conner and Stewart Kellerman's Grammarphobia (grammarphobia.com)
Jonathon Owen's Arrant Pedantry (arrantpedantry.com)

Kory Stamper's Harmless Drudgery
   (korystamper.wordpress.com)
Online Etymology Dictionary (etymonline.com)
Mignon Fogarty's Quick and Dirty Tips
   (quickanddirtytips.com/grammar-girl)
Stan Carey's Sentence First (stancarey.wordpress
   .com)
John McIntyre's You Don't Say (baltimoresun
   .com/news/language-blog)

ACKNOWLEDGMENTS

I would like to express my gratitude to everyone at Delacorte Press for their enthusiastic labor on and support of this specially youthened edition of *Dreyer's English,* especially publisher Beverly Horowitz, Colleen Fellingham, Alison Kolani, Tamar Schwartz, Nathan Kinney, Katrina Damkoehler, Ken Crossland, Rebecca Gudelis, and the Random House Children's Books teams in Publicity; Trade, School & Library, and Digital Marketing; and Sales.

INDEX

ABOUT THE AUTHOR

Benjamin Dreyer is vice president, executive managing editor and copy chief, of Random House. He has copyedited books by authors including E. L. Doctorow, David Ebershoff, Frank Rich, and Elizabeth Strout, as well as *Let Me Tell You,* a volume of previously unpublished and uncollected work by Shirley Jackson. A graduate of Northwestern University, he lives in New York City.

@BCDREYER